D1098384

What the world's leading author of business best-sellers is saying about The One Page Business Plan®...

"The One Page Business Plan is an out-and-out winner. Period.

It makes great sense to me as a so-called *business thinker.* But the acid test was applying it to a start-up I co-founded. We spent several days drafting our one pager — and have been editing it ever since. It is a powerful, living document; the very nature of which has led us to important new insights.

The One Page Business Plan = the proverbial better mouse trap!"

— Tom Peters

author of
In Search of Excellence,
Thriving on Chaos,
Liberation Management,
The Pursuit of Wow!
and *The Circle of Innovation*

WITHDRAWN

What Others Are Saying

The One Page Business Plan® takes a complex process and makes it simple!

"I've had a number of business plans, but none of them were effective. Having all the essentials of our plan on one page helped get me and my partners on track!"

Norman Kurtin, Design Media, Inc.

"The friendly visual graphics, and the no-nonsense approach to business planning got me over my reluctance to write a business plan. This process got me to think out of the box and to create my dream business! Now I have a great plan and it's working."

Kendall Moalem, Kendall Moalem Design

"My board of advisors applauded my one page business plan. They finally understood my business and are contributing important advice because they have a written plan to review."

Nicole Lazzaro, President, XEODesign, Inc.

"I was too busy developing plans for clients to complete my own, but a one page business plan of key words and short phrases seemed so easy and "doable" that I wrote one immediately!"

Diane Weinsheimer, The Marketing Manager

"I have been writing the same goals and visions for my business over and over. What I wrote in March, I wrote in June, and again in September. After I heard Jim speak, I wrote my one page plan. I now choose my opportunities more wisely and waste less time because I have my plan in place."

Linda Pollock, Professional Organizer

"The One Page Business Plan is the business owner's Cliff Notes."

Fred DaMert, Chairman, DaMert Company

"This is an innovative, fresh approach to business planning. If all loan applicants would provide us with clear, concise summaries of their business plan, a banker's life would be a lot easier."

Jim Ryan, Chairman, Bank of Walnut Creek, California

"As a banker, I love The One Page Business Plan. I know the potential business owner is serious, committed and professional. This is truly a breakthrough in business planning!"

Jerry Ricketts, Vice President, Scotts Valley Bank

"The One Page Business Plan truly helps the prospective entrepreneur or existing business owner get focused and clear on one page. When they are clear on one page, they have a much better chance for success!"

Greg Garrett, Program Manager, One Stop Capital Shop

"It's easy for a stockbroker to get wrapped up in the market and lose perspective that you are in business for yourself. In order to be successful for the long run, one must have a plan and The One Page Business Plan is a great tool."

Ralph Miljanich, Vice President, Dean Witter Reynolds, Inc.

"It's wonderful that someone finally came up with a business plan for independent professionals. It de-mystifies business planning so that the average business professional can actually write a business plan that makes sense!"

Rebecca Salome Shaw, Entrepreneurial Authors

"The One Page Business Plan revolutionizes business planning! It cuts the fluff and the filler and gets right to the point. This is a powerful tool for businesses of all sizes!"

Roger McAniff, Sage Consulting

The One Page Business Plan®

Start with a vision, build a company!

by

Jim Horan

Adapted for the UK

by

Paul Barrow

LRC Stoke Park
GUILDFORD COLLEGE

CAPSTONE

658.4012 HOR
157144
7 day
CD available, please ask at Issue Desk

Copyright © 2008 by Jim Horan

Adapted from the original version published in the United States by The One Page Business Plan Company, The One Page Business Plan for the Creative Entrepreneur, James T. Horan, Jr.

This edition published by Capstone Publishing Ltd. (a Wiley Company).
The Atrium, Southern Gate, Chichester, PO19 8SQ, UK.
www.wileyeurope.com

Email (for orders and customer service enquires): cs-books@wiley.co.uk

The right of Jim Horan to be identified as the author of this book has been asserted in accordance with the Copyright, Designs and Patents Act 1988.

The One Page and The One Page Business Plan are registered trademarks of The One Page Business Plan Company.

All Rights Reserved. No part of this publication may be reproduced, stored in a retrieval system or transmitted in any form or by any means, electronic, mechanical, photocopying,recording, scanning or otherwise, except under the terms of the Copyright, Designs and Patents Act 1988 or under the terms of a licence issued by the Copyright Licensing Agency Ltd, 90 Tottenham Court Road, London W1T 4LP, UK, without the permission in writing of the Publisher. Requests to the Publisher should be addressed to the Permissions Department, John Wiley & Sons Ltd, The Atrium, Southern Gate, Chichester, West Sussex PO19 8SQ, England, or emailed to permreq@wiley.co.uk, or faxed to (+44) 1243 770571.

Designations used by companies to distinguish their products are often claimed as trademarks. All brand names and product names used in this book are trade names, service marks, trademarks or registered trademarks of their respective owners. The Publisher is not associated with any product or vendor mentioned in this book.

This publication is designed to provide accurate and authoritative information in regard to the subject matter covered. It is sold on the understanding that the Publisher is not engaged in rendering professional services. If professional advice or other expert assistance is required, the services of a competent professional should be sought.

Other Wiley Editorial Offices

John Wiley & Sons Inc., 111 River Street, Hoboken, NJ 07030, USA
Jossey-Bass, 989 Market Street, San Francisco, CA 94103-1741, USA
Wiley-VCH Verlag GmbH, Boschstr. 12, D-69469 Weinheim, Germany
John Wiley & Sons Australia Ltd, 42 McDougall Street, Milton, Queensland 4064, Australia
John Wiley & Sons (Asia) Pte Ltd, 2 Clementi Loop #02-01, Jin Xing Distripark, Singapore 129809
John Wiley & Sons Canada Ltd, 22 Worcester Road, Etobicoke, Ontario, Canada M9W 1L1

Wiley also publishes its books in a variety of electronic formats. Some content that appears in print may not be available in electronic books.

A catalogue record for this book is available from the British Library.

ISBN 13: 978-1-90646-531-5

Typeset by Macmillan Publishing Solutions, Chennai, India
Printed and bound in TJ International Ltd, Padstow, Cornwall, UK

Substantial discounts on bulk quantities of Capstone Books are available to corporations, professional associations and other organisations. For details telephone John Wiley & Sons on (+44) 1243-770441, fax (+44) 1243 770571 or email corporatedevelopment@ wiley.co.uk

This book is dedicated to the
family, friends, and the extended
community that supports and
nurtures entrepreneurs.

Without their love and support,
many entrepreneurs would not be able to make
their dreams come true.

Acknowledgments

I never dreamed I would write a book. This has been one of the hardest things I have ever tackled, and it is one of the most gratifying. This book would never have been completed without the assistance, guidance, and professionalism of two wonderful people, Ruthie Petty of Designwise, my book designer and Roger McAniff of Sage Consulting, a long time friend and fellow consultant. They both went the extra mile again and again to keep me on track to make sure this endeavor was completed.

The road to completion was long and windy. Many people provided important services, too many to list them all. Early on Marie Krakow focused me with the outline and Emily Marks turned my initial thoughts on the graphics into wonderful prototypes. My editor, Rebecca Salome Shaw kept me on track thoughout and polished the words and sentences along the way. I truly thank each one of them.

Catherine Marshall, founder of the San Francisco Bay Area Entreprenuers Association deserves special recognition for her pioneering work in entrepreneurship. Her programs have helped to build many successful businesses in the San Francisco Bay Area. Her contribution and the contribution of my fellow BAEA members to my personal and business development have been immense.

Special thanks to Ron Forney and Peg Bogle, my newsletter partners. The lessons learned from four years of publishing a quarterly newsletter have been immense. Ron and Peg have been great supporters!

I am also very thankful to my family, friends, clients, business associates and the many wonderful entrepreneurs who have supported me in my dream. Their encouragement has been continuous and heartfelt.

UK Edition Acknowledgements

The publishing of this book, The One Page Business Plan, UK Edition is due to the highly creative and professional talents of the Wiley/Capstone publishing team starting with Jenny Ng, Assistant Editor, Grace O'Byrne, Content Editor, Sarah Sutton, Executive Commissioning Editor and Iain Campbell, Senior Marketing Manager.

I would also like to express a very genuine thank you to Paul Barrow for adapting and localizing this edition for the UK market. His contribution was significant.

We would like to thank the BBC and Blackwell Publishing for the excellent Mission Statements they have created for their companies. We have included these statements because of their excellence and the fine example they provide for young fledgling businesses.

Author's Note

"You must simplify.

You must make the complex simple, then you must make it work."

— I. M. Pei
Master Architect

There is a new breed of business owner in the marketplace today. These business owners are either starting up new businesses or reinventing established businesses. These individuals are intensely passionate and strategic. They are very competitive and heartfull. They care about people, the environment, and their communities. They do not run their businesses casually. They are professional entrepreneurs.

There is also another type of entrepreneur, the accidental entrepreneur. These individuals are finding themselves considering self-employment for the first time in their lives.

I know the accidental entrepreneur very well, I happen to be one. I came kicking and screaming into the world of entrepreneurship in 1990 after spending 17 years in Fortune 500 companies as a senior financial executive. In 1990, I began a search for my next career. I found myself self-employed, as a business and financial advisor, drawn to working with entrepreneurs and independent business owners.

Today, my company is a broad-based consulting company serving professional and accidental entrepreneurs, executives and business owners. Client companies are in a wide range of industries large and small.

All these companies share similar issues. Business is complex, resources are limited, and time is of the essence. There is no room for big mistakes. Business owners can't know it all and can't do it all by themselves. Therefore, other people will become involved in the business. That means employees, independent contractors, investors, and potentially partners. Additionally, your business may require the use of "other people's money." Other people and "other people's money" necessitate having a written business plan. It's no longer optional.

The One Page Business Plan® was inspired by my work with entrepreneurs. These individuals like to think fast and move fast, and the concept of a traditional business plan was out of the question. An innovative, fresh approach to business planning was required, and the One Page Business Plan® was born.

The One Page Business Plan® is designed to act as a catalyst for your ideas. It's a powerful tool for building and managing a business in the 21st century. It's short, it's concise, and it delivers your plan quickly and effectively. There can be no question as to where you are going when it's in writing. Start with your vision, build a company.

— Jim Horan

Contents

Author's Note **7**
How to Use This Book **11**
How to Use the CD **13**

1 Introduction **17**
The One Page Business Plan® 17
Uses of the One Page Business Plan® 19
The Power and Magic of Writing 21
Modelling the New Idea 23
Why the One Page Business Plan® Works 25
Building a Business Is a Journey 27

2 The Vision Statement **29**
Brainstorm Exercise: Creating the Company You Want 30
Interview Exercise 32
Focus Exercise: Crafting Your Vision Statement 33
Examples of Vision Statements that Work 34
Feedback Exercise 36
Summarise 37

3 The Mission Statement **39**
Brainstorm Exercise: What's in it for the customer and you? 40
Interview Exercise 42
Focus Exercise: Crafting Your Mission Statement 43
Examples of Mission Statements 44
Feedback Exercise 46
Summarise 47

4 The Objectives 49
Brainstorm Exercise: What accomplishments would you like to celebrate? 50
Brainstorm Exercise: Where does success come from? What will it look like? 51
Focus Exercise: What targets will you aim for? 52
Focus Exercise: What does this business need to accomplish? 54
Focus Exercise: Crafting Meaningful Objectives 55
Examples of Objectives 56
Summarise 57

5 The Strategies 59
Brainstorm Exercise: Key Elements to Building Your Business 60
Decide Which Strategies are Appropriate for Your Business 60
Research Exercise: Opportunities and Threats 61
Focus Exercise: Who are your customers? How will you promote and sell to them? . 62
Brainstorm Exercise: What's working in your company? 64
Focus Exercise: Critical Issues Examination 65
Focus Exercise: How do we get from here to there? 66
Focus Exercise: Crafting Meaningful Strategies 67
Examples of Strategies 68
Summarise 69

6 The Plans 71
Brainstorm Exercise: Business-Building Projects 72
Focus Exercise: Integrating Objectives, Strategies, and Plans 74
Focus Exercise: Crafting Meaningful Plans 75
Examples of Plans 76
Summarise 77

7 You Did It! 79
Polishing Checklist 80
Putting the Plan into Action 81
One Page Business Plan® Samples 83

Business Plan Myths

- All business plans are in writing.
- They must be long to be good.
- Their primary purpose is to obtain financing.
- It's easier for others to do business plans.
- You can and should do it all by yourself.
- It takes six months, a significant amount of the owner's and key staff members' time, and expensive consultants.
- If completed, it will sit unused on a bookshelf.
- My business is too small; business plans are for big businesses.
- I know where I'm taking my business, I do not need a written business plan.
- I can just pay to have a consultant write it for me, and that will be good enough.

Let's dispel the myths.

How to Use This Book

The primary purpose of this book is to help you get your business plan onto paper. It has been carefully crafted to capture the business plan that is in your head.

Carry this book with you, write in it, use it as a container for capturing your thoughts as they occur. If you have multiple businesses, buy a book for each one.

It's not necessary to do all the exercises in this book. If you can write your One Page Business Plan® by reviewing the samples — skip the exercises. They are there to help guide you through the process if you need help.

This book does not look like the typical business planning book — it isn't intended to. The exercises and examples are meant to stimulate you. The graphics and images are meant to guide you. If they look playful, be playful and explore. If they look analytical, be analytical and focused. The examples and samples are from real business plans. They are meant to show you how powerful a few words or a well-constructed phrase can be.

Not all people think or work the same way. Some are auditory; others respond visually; some need to write. Some do their best thinking alone, silently. Others do their best thinking out loud. This book has been designed to accommodate all of these different styles.

Do not underestimate the power of the questions in this book that appear simple! They are simple by design. That's so you will understand them. If you do not get an "aha" from them, have somebody ask you the questions. Important insights may begin to flow.

This book is divided into seven sections with the focus on the five elements of The One Page Business Plan®. You can start anywhere. It's OK to jump around!

There are five types of exercises in the book. They are clearly marked and identified at the top of each page with these icons. Each type of exercise is designed to achieve a specific purpose:

- **Brainstorming —** generate new ideas by considering provocative questions
- **Research —** gather information from external sources
- **Focusing —** process of prioritising ideas and concepts
- **Summarising —** condensing, final prioritising, editing
- **Feedback —** solicit objective feedback from trusted advisors

There are many different ways to use and interact with this book. Exercises can be done:

- by oneself
- with a planning partner (one business owner working with another business owner)
- as a management team
- as a group — feedback exercise (one business owner receiving input from several business owners or professionals)
- by a group of entrepreneurs or business owners for brainstorming business planning concepts, ideas, strategies
- with a professional business consultant

Some final thoughts…

There is no right, wrong, or perfect business plan. Your business will always be evolving. So will your plan. It will also get better with time. Remember, it is not necessary to do all the exercises in this book nor is it desirable to do it all by yourself. Use this book as a catalyst. When you think you are finished, stop. If you get stuck, put it aside for a few days or a week. Come back to it when the ideas start to flow. Take your time and enjoy the journey.

How to Use the CD

The Entrepreneur's Toolkit CD contains additional tools to make the creation of your business plan simple and easy.

Some Useful Stuff

Now that we have whetted your appetite you will probably find that using the interactive exercises and templates on the CD will speed up the process of preparing your business plan and help preserve your book. Also using the sales calculators and one page budget worksheets will help you get to grips with the underlying numbers. You will find the bonus tools really useful in working out key things like your marketing plan. Just for good measure we have included some sample business plans, to give you an idea how a similar business has prepared theirs. Finally we have given you some tools to help you to control your business as you start to deliver your new business plan. I bet you can't wait to get started.

What's on the CD?

The CD has 6 folders:

- Interactive Exercises and Templates
- Sales Calculators
- Budget Worksheets
- Sample Plans
- Scorecards
- Bonus Tools

Don't forget you will need both Microsoft Excel and Word to open and use all of this content.

So What's What?

Interactive Exercises and Templates

You will probably want to start with the Interactive Exercises and Templates first as these are duplicated from the book. Don't forget that as you work through the book you will see a **symbol** at the foot of the pages that have an equivalent on the CD. The file names on the CD relate to the specific pages in the book so they are easy to find. Most of the forms, templates and exercises have text boxes that you can type directly into.

Sales Calculators

You will then probably want to prepare a sales forecast for the period of your business plan. You don't need to be a CPA, MBA, or Marketing Guru to get a sense of what your sales might look like in 1, 3, or 5 years. To help you there are 5 Excel spreadsheets.

- **Sales Budget** – Sample: This is an example of a multi product (upto 7 products) 12 month sales forecast. Each product can have variable monthly selling and cost prices.
- **Sales Budget System:** The real life version of the Sample above. Use this to prepare your 12 month multi product sales forecast.
- **12 Month Sales Calculator:** A simple monthly sales forecast suitable for single product businesses. It contains an example to show you how to complete it.
- **60 Month Sales Calculator:** This is a simple forecasting tool that extrapolates your monthly sales figures on a monthly basis for 5 years assuming a monthly starting sales volume figure, a monthly % growth factor, and an average selling price. It contains an example to show you how to complete it.
- **5 Year Sales Calculator:** This is a simple forecasting tool that extrapolates your annual sales figures on an annual basis for 5 years assuming an annual starting sales value, an annual % growth factor. It can accommodate up to 7 different products. It contains an example to show you how to complete it.

Each Sales Calculator has one or more colourful, easy-to-read graphs to help you visualise the growth of your business in addition to seeing the actual numbers. This is a great tool for entrepreneurs who have been intimidated by the 'numbers' associated with business!

Budget Worksheets

After you have done your sales forecast, it is time to estimate your expenses and calculate your profit. The next stage would be to run your sales figures through the following 2 Excel spreadsheets.

- **One Page Budget Worksheet:** This is a simple annual budget sheet into which you can enter your monthly sales figures (see earlier) and your monthly company costs of goods sold and overheads. There are models for businesses with or without costs of goods sold (COGS). Also there are sample worksheets for manufacturing, service, and professional service businesses to guide you.

Interactive Exercises and Templates

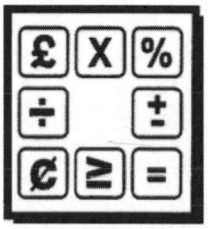

Sales Calculators

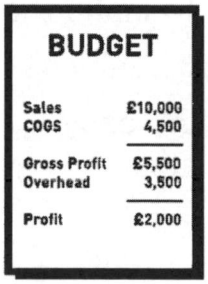

Budget Worksheets

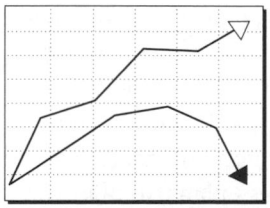

Scorecards

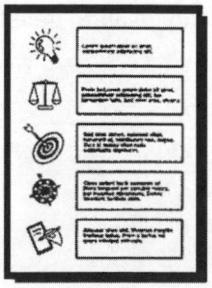

Sample Plans

- **Breakeven Analysis:** A very simple representation of when your business will break even based on your monthly sales and costs, which you will have already worked out in the spreadsheet above.

Sample Plans

Having done everything so far you may just like to compare your One Page Business Plan to some others. There are 19 sample One Page Business Plans to compare it with from different business sectors, different sizes, etc. – just to see if you are on the right lines.

Scorecards

So now that you have got your plan in place it is time to get on that journey. To make sure you stay on course you need some tools to help you. This collection of Excel worksheets gives you everything you need to monitor the key areas of your business. We encourage you to create a Scorecard for each Objective and update them monthly.

- **Performance Scorecard:** Complete one of these for every performance measure you want to monitor, e.g., Sales, Gross Margin, Number of New Clients Gained, Sales per employee. Enter the figures each month and it will graph your actual performance against budget, forecast, and last year.
- **Sample Accounts Rec(eivable):** A sample spreadsheet which graphically shows actual monthly Debtor Days against budget, forecast, and last year.
- **Sample Billable Hours:** As above but used to monitor billable hours.
- **Sample Production Units:** As above but used to monitor production output.
- **Sample Profit Before Tax:** As above but used to monitor profit before tax.
- **Sample Sales Scorecard:** As above but used to monitor sales
- **Sample Units Sold:** As above but used to monitor units of product sold.

Bonus Tools

To make sure that what you have done so far is looking good, why not check out these Word documents that show you 5 one page worksheets?

- One Page Marketing Plan
- One Page Objectives Worksheet with Graphs
- One Page Plan Template with Fill in the Gaps
- One Page Plan Template with Instructions
- One Page Planning Wheel

Also there are some more sample documents to help you:

- Bend The Curve: Shows the linkage between Strategies, Plans and Objectives
- Business Assessment Worksheet: A simple scoring system to rate how well your company is doing
- Sample Vision & Mission Statement by Function/Division
- Strategy Development – Fill in the blanks: A simple Aid Memoir to articulate a range of strategies
- Vision & Mission by Department Worksheet: A blank version of the earlier sample Vision & Mission Statement by function/division for you to complete

Introducing

The One Page Business Plan®

Hampshire Garden Window Company

2009 Business Plan Summary

Become recognised as the leader in designing and manufacturing custom and replacement garden windows and skylights.

Vision

How do you visualise your company in the future?

Bring light, air and the beauty of nature into homes through creative windows!

Mission

Why does this business exist?

- Achieve 2009 sales of £17 million with £1.5 million in pretax profits.
- Grow garden window division at 8% per year and achieve £5.3 million in 2009.
- Expand skylight/custom window product lines; grow sales to £7.5 million in 2009.
- Implement profit improvement programs & reduce product cost to 38%.
- Reduce distribution costs to 4% of sales through facility consolidation & technology.
- Reduce inventory levels to 3.3 months by August 31st.
- Achieve 98% ontime delivery with 98% order accuracy in 1st quarter.

Objectives

What accomplishments must this business achieve within one year to be successful?

- Focus on new upscale home developments & baby-boomer remodelling trends.
- Build Hampshire Garden Window into nationally-recognised brand name.
- Become vendor-of-choice by maintaining inventory of standard window sizes.
- Control quality by manufacturing in-house.
- Increase capacity by minimising duplicate products & increasing mfg. efficiencies.
- Centralise distribution into one location; reducing costs, improving service.

Strategies

How will this business be built and managed over time?

- Introduce new Scenic Garden Windows at SF Products Show (March 2009).
- Hire new sales rep by April; focus on Signature Homes in Southampton and Portsmouth.
- Implement new MRP software by July 31st to achieve inventory reduction.
- Complete skylight product rationalisation program by Aug. 15th.
- Phase in new packaging design beginning March 31st.
- Complete employee benefit program redesign by Sept. 30th.

Plans

What specific projects and actions will be taken this year to achieve the objectives?

Introduction

The One Page Business Plan®

Visionaries are the keepers of the dreams.

Entrepreneurs take risks and make the dreams real.

The community nurtures and supports creative businesses.

Every business owner has a business plan. Meet a business owner at a party and most likely you will hear the majority of that plan within 30 minutes. Of course they will boast about their latest product success, and moan about employees, customers, and partner problems. If you listen, you'll also hear them freely describe their vision, objectives, strategies, and their plans.

Business plans don't have to be long to be good. A single page can contain all of the essential elements you need to tell your employees, board of directors, potential partners, or banker where you are taking your business and how you are going to get there. This book is going to show you how to do that.

The most important reason to have a business plan is to clarify your thinking, regardless of the size of your company. Is it possible to have too much clarity or focus? How much of your time and your business resources are wasted on projects that detract from your primary mission? What could you accomplish if everyone in your organisation really knew what you were trying to do? To have a business plan is to be clear about where you are taking your business. When you're clear, and it's in writing, others will know and understand your vision and how you plan to get there.

Extensive business plans are required by those people and organisations who have money that you want. They have specific requirements that must be met or you will not get their money. This book is not about those business plans, but can greatly simplify their preparation. If you can get focused and clear on one page, you can then turn each short phrase into a paragraph, a full page, a chapter, etc. It is always easy to expand, it's much more difficult to focus and simplify. Mark Twain once said, "give me three weeks and I'll write you a short letter."

It doesn't have to take six months of agonising meetings, pounds of written documents, endless spreadsheets, and complicated flowcharts to produce a meaningful business plan. It also does not take an army of expensive consultants. A few well-constructed phrases and short sentences can say a lot. The examples in this book will demonstrate that for you.

You and your team know your business, inside and out. You know your industry — the major trends. You talk with your competitors and suppliers regularly. You read the newspaper, and trade journals, and maybe even surf the net a little. You also share your dreams with your close friends, associates, and family. You have everything you need to draft the plan in your head. You could draft it this morning and have a meaningful discussion with someone you trust this afternoon. If you want to bring in a consultant to help, great! Give them a copy of your draft and interview them. If they have valuable insights, hire them and have them help you refine it.

"The most important reason to have a business plan is to clarify your thinking, regardless of the size of your company."

Business planning concepts are not difficult. You already understand all of them. You dream about your business, you set goals, and you work throughout the year in an organised manner to make it all happen. You probably would like to do it with less stress and better results. That's why the concept of a one page plan sounds good to you.

Why must you have a written plan? You know where you are going. But without a written plan, it's always subject to change. Every time you talk about it, it will be different. Put it in writing and everyone sees the same thing.

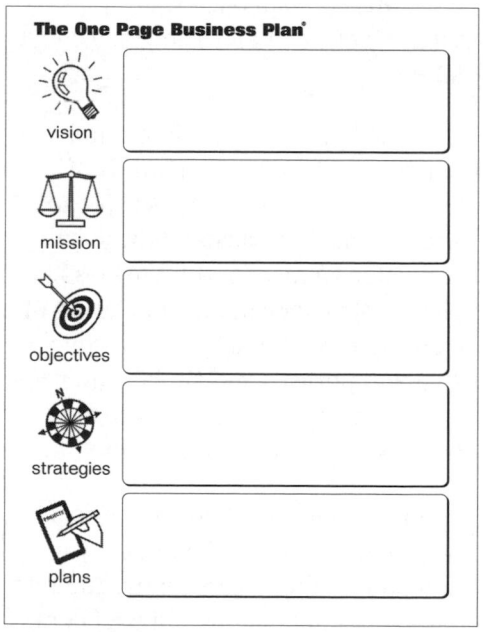

If writing a business plan still seems too big of a task, even after reading this book, get another business owner to commit to doing his or her plan at the same time. It's kind of like going to the health club with a friend. Get a planning partner, commit to a process, and set some deadlines. Serve as coach and cheerleader to your planning partner. It works. I know because I got writer's block when I attempted to write my own. A fellow entrepreneur gently but firmly guided and challenged me through the process. I did the same for him.

A business plan brings out the best and worst in most business professionals. It facilitates creative and analytical thinking, problem solving, communications, interfunctional sharing, and teamwork. It generates hope and enthusiasm about the future. It also brings out procrastination, frustration, differences of opinions, and possibly anger. It is not a benign process. But when done well, the process is very valuable and has its own sense of satisfaction. Your business will be stronger.

Uses of The One Page Business Plan®

There are many uses for the One Page Business Plan.® Listed below are four categories with many different uses. This list is obviously not exhaustive but meant to give you an idea of some of its uses to date. Keep blank copies of the One Page Business Plan® handy. If you find yourself dreaming about a new product, service, business, or career, start taking notes. Capture your thoughts as they come.

External Presentation

- Complete business plan for small to mid-size companies
- Vehicle for testing business ideas with your board of directors, partners, banker, and employees
- Draft concept for Small Business Administration loan or venture capital funding business plan
- Summarises existing plan

Inspiration and Motivation

- Tool to get back on track if you've lost your vision
- Career planning

Research and Development

- Place to summarise ideas for new division or new business
- Quick sketch and fleshing out of idea for new product or service
- Process for planning major projects

Internal Process Guide

- Complete business plan for small to mid-size companies
- Business plan for subsidiaries or divisions of larger corporations
- Functional or departmental planning tool (sales, marketing, finance, etc.)
- Strategic planning starting point for CEOs in larger corporations
- Methodology to quickly update annual plan for significant mid-year changes
- Summarises existing plan

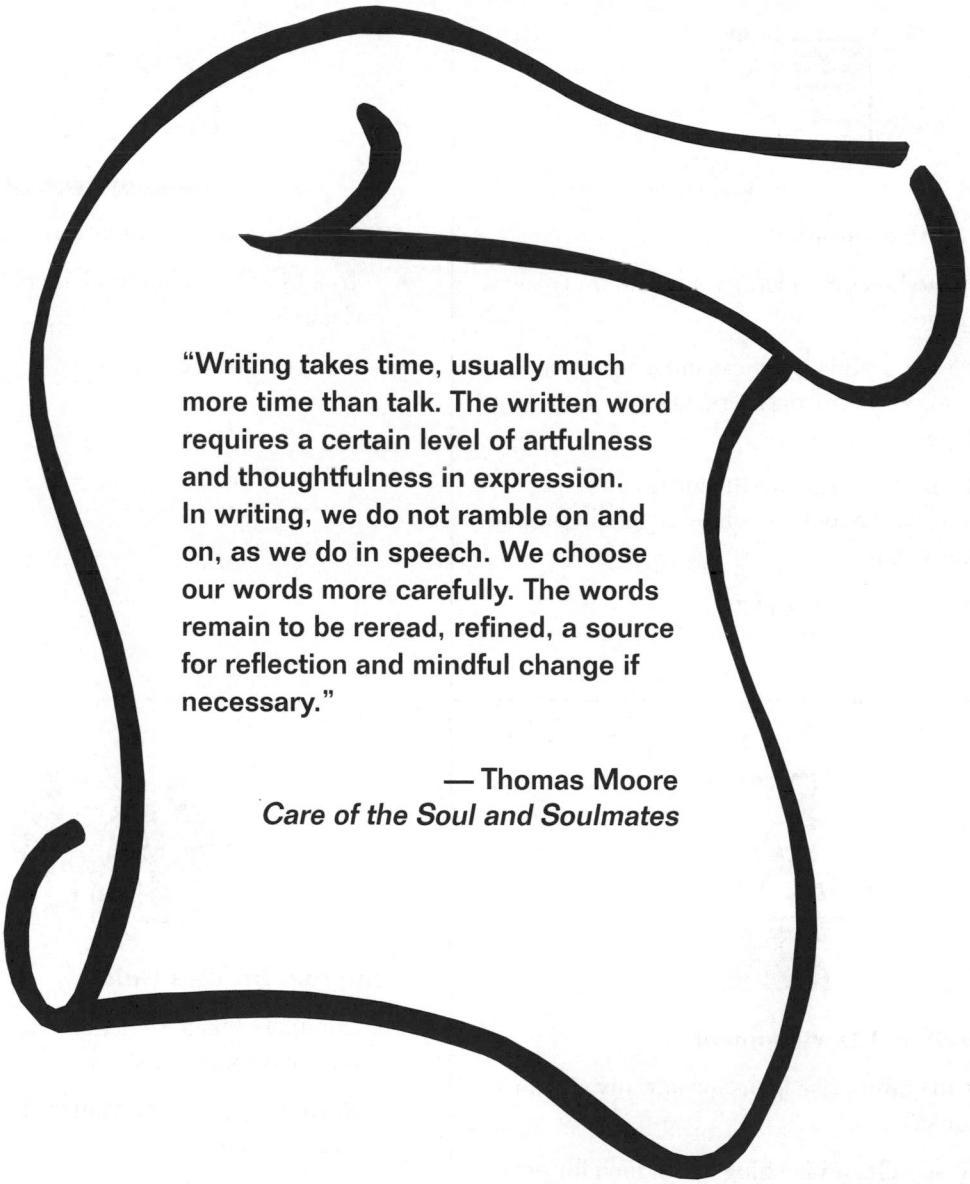

"Writing takes time, usually much more time than talk. The written word requires a certain level of artfulness and thoughtfulness in expression. In writing, we do not ramble on and on, as we do in speech. We choose our words more carefully. The words remain to be reread, refined, a source for reflection and mindful change if necessary."

— Thomas Moore
Care of the Soul and Soulmates

The Power and Magic of Writing

There is magic in the written word! Especially when they're your words about an idea that you have been thinking and talking about for sometime. Somehow the process of writing initiates the transformation from idea to reality. It also does many other wonderful things.

Things get clearer when you write. Of course at first the process can feel very awkward, and the results seem poor and anything but clear. But given time and patience, the process results in a connection of the mind with the reality of the paper. Thoughts begin to develop into images. Images turn into key words and short phrases. An outline begins to emerge, and the clarity builds.

If you stick with your writing, you also get focused. In the beginning, you'll have many ideas, more than you can ever implement. But the process of capturing them on paper results in a conscious and unconscious ranking and prioritisation. I believe it is important to capture as many of your thoughts regarding your product, service, or business as possible without critiquing them. The natural process of writing will keep the best and strongest of your ideas. Your vision and mission will become more concise through this evolutionary process, resulting in a focused approach.

"Writing allows others to participate in your dream and give you feedback."

Writing allows others to participate in your dream and give you feedback. Writing provides a consistent forum, whereas in conversation the context changes each time you speak. Allowing others to participate and help support your idea to its next step is crucial to your overall success. The lone ranger mentality is no longer necessary nor effective.

The written word also produces a contract with yourself that results in immediate action. Haven't you found that if you make up a grocery list and leave it at home you almost always remember everything on the list? Many users of The One Page Business Plan® report that as soon as they begin to write their action items — some of which they have been thinking about for years — they start to take action on them. I think it's magic!

1. Architects visualise the details of a new building and produce a simple sketch to see how it might look.

2. Songwriters mentally hear a new melody and then test it out on a piano to see how it will sound.

3. Movie producers imagine the setting of their next picture and produce story-boards to help them produce a more complete image of their story.

Modelling the New Idea

"...business owners need a way to test their ideas without having to put their cash or business at high risk."

Architects, songwriters, movie producers, and inventors make models in some shape or form so they can see their ideas in a more visual, concrete manner. This process is one of the early steps that makes an idea something real and tangible. Models are a technique to help with the visualisation of ideas.

As creators of businesses, we need a methodology for exploring our business ideas. It's too difficult, expensive, and nonproductive to produce working models or samples for every potential idea that comes our way. Market research is also very expensive and is generally reserved for our very best ideas. Complicated products with long lead times, requiring expensive raw materials and manufacturing facilities, obviously cannot be produced and tested like a new melody on the piano. And yet business owners need a way to test their ideas without having to put their cash or business at high risk.

Most individuals in business check out their ideas in conversation with trusted associates, consultants, friends, and relatives. But conversation is fluid, flexible, and frequently informal. Also we may not deliver the same message and details to everyone; hence the response we receive may be affected by the way we presented our thoughts. A melody played from written music will sound similar regardless of the piano it's played on. Unfortunately the spoken word is subject to much greater ambiguity when delivered.

Business people do, however, have the written word to describe their thoughts and ideas. The written word allows the sharing of our ideas with others in a consistent, clear fashion. The business plan is, in effect, our modelling tool. It provides the sketch, the vision, the road map for our ideas. In many ways, it's just like the composer's first few chords; the musician gets to hear it and so do others. The business plan works the same way. You get to see your ideas in writing and so do others.

INTERVIEW EXERCISE

Ask your planning partner or a fellow business owner to interview you with the questions below. Tape the session so both of you can take notes from the recorder afterwards. Then write each person's notes below. ⌛ 30 minutes

Describe your business. Where are you going with it? What will it look like in five years?

What market need will your company's product or service fulfill? Why are you in this business? What's your passion?

What would you like to celebrate this year? What would you like to celebrate this time, next year?

What has made your business successful to date? What will make your business successful over time?

What business-building projects are on your to-do list? What have you been procrastinating on that you know would make a difference in your business?

Why The One Page Business Plan® Works

Business plans don't have to be complex and cumbersome. The One Page Business Plan® is meant to be simple and to help you get focused quickly.

Simplicity

The One Page Business Plan® is effective because it takes a complex subject and makes it simple. It's easy to read and understand. If you are the writer, you will know when you are finished because you have effectively covered all of the important elements of your business plan.

Focus

The One Page Business Plan® works because it focuses on what's important. There is no room for fluff or filler. The use of key words and short phrases tells your reader that only the essence is being presented for review. The fact that this business plan is only one page communicates that the investment in reading is limited.

Readily Understandable

The five elements of the One Page Business Plan® are readily understandable. As you read each section, the business plan element telegraphs the kind of information being presented. You know the vision statement is going to be expansive and idealistic. You expect the mission statement to be powerful and customer oriented. Objectives should be realistic and measurable. Strategies are well thought out, and plans are action oriented.

Versatility

The One Page Business Plan® works because it's a tool for communication. If you are the owner of a business, this one page document can be an important tool for communicating to your existing or prospective employees, partners, shareholders, investors, or banker the kind of company you are building and how you plan to build it.

Consistency

It's an effective communication tool because you send the same message to every person you give it to — unlike the spoken word, which may change every time you speak. Additionally, with the written word, you have chosen your words carefully and you are communicating only the most important elements of your business plan.

Flexibility

The One Page Business Plan® works because it's easy to change and update with your latest thinking. An important thought in the morning can be in your plan that afternoon. Capturing those "moments of clarity" quickly and in a useful manner will preserve them for further review, consideration, and possible action.

So what's the benefit of having a One Page Plan? It's your plan, your ideas, in your words. It's a reference point for any significant business or financial decision you may be considering. It's simple, concise, and it's you. Bankers, investors, and potential partners can have a complete overview of your business at a glance. Attach your budget and you're ready for a meaningful discussion about your business.

"Had you considered that Queen Isabella of Spain was one of the most powerful and important venture capitalists of all time?"

Building a Business Is a Journey...

The business plan is your map!

Building a business is a journey, it always has been. Marco Polo, Christopher Columbus, and Ferdinand Magellan were all great adventurers who took extended journeys. These journeys were explorations into the unknown parts of the world seeking new lands, exotic spices, fame, and fortune. These explorers were also businessmen and many of them had venture capitalists. Had you considered that Queen Isabella of Spain was one of the most powerful and important venture capitalists of all time?

Great journeys start with a vision. The vision is the dream. It describes what the journey is about and what you hope to find or create. Columbus's vision was to reach the Indies by sailing west.

All great journeys also have a mission. The mission describes the purpose for the trip. Columbus wanted to prove the world was round. Queen Isabella's mission was different. She wanted the riches and the power that conquering the new lands would bring.

Journeys have specific goals or objectives that drive certain behaviour. John F. Kennedy wanted to have a man on the moon by the end of the 1960s. This goal focused many people's energy into specific actions to achieve this deadline. That's the purpose of a well-defined objective; it produces meaningful action.

Strategies set the direction. They are the road signs. They help to keep you on target so that you ultimately achieve your destination. Great strategies remain constant over the entire journey; Columbus kept heading west and it worked! Establish clear strategies for building and growing your business and stick to them.

Successful journeys have a plan. The plan details the important actions that must be taken to make the venture a success.

Wherever you are, today is the starting point. Develop a business plan that guides the building of your business. Use your business plan as a map to keep you on track to your destination.

A Vision Statement That Works:

To build Universal Electronic Controls, plc. into the premier industrial process control company in the Southwest.

Within five years grow UEC, plc. to £20 million in revenues by expanding its role from a manufacturing representative business to a value-added company offering complete engineering, field service, and integration engineering services.

The Vision Statement

How do you visualise your business?

"The Vision Statement should describe your idea in a manner that captures the passion of the idea."

The vision section of The One Page Business Plan® is very important. It's the place where you get to describe your vision, your way! Vision statements should be expansive and idealistic. They should stimulate thinking, communicate passion, and paint a very graphic picture of the business you want. Great vision statements are fun to read. When written well, they can trigger emotional and sensory reactions. If perchance you are looking for investors, a great vision statement is essential.

There is another important reason to create a large vision. When you describe your vision in an expanded manner, you are inviting others to help you see possibilities you might not see. I believe vision statements are all about exploration, creating possibilities, and asking "what if" and "why not."

You can hardly exaggerate your vision statement. Go ahead and write a wildly optimistic, no limits, maybe even outrageous, vision statement. Ask your friends and associates to push you to think "way out of the box." Then live with what you wrote for a while. Don't rush into the editing process. It may just turn out that you decide to build something more exciting than you originally believed possible.

Don't sanitise your vision statement. Keep it full of passion. This is your opportunity to describe your dream. This section of the business plan is not the place to be analytical. If you describe a limited vision, one that is dull and boring, how can you expect to be excited about your business? And if you aren't excited, how can you expect to be successful? If you don't capture the passion you feel, others will have difficulty getting interested in your project. In fact, investors typically say that the dream is almost always worth more than the reality.

The key to capturing your vision is to be free flowing and not to restrict the flow of any thoughts. Capture all thoughts that come to your mind and use powerful adjectives to describe all the characteristics. Be sure to include the personal elements of your vision, as this is the source of your passion that will carry you through the difficult and frustrating times.

Your vision has evolved over time and will continue to change. Don't allow future ideas to impede your writing today. Describe your vision as you see it now!

BRAINSTORM

EXERCISE

Your Vision...

As you think about the questions on these two pages, write down any words or short phrases that come to mind in the "idea balloons" below.

WHAT?

Products or services? or both? How many?

Company Image: What will this company be known for?

Owner's Role: What is your role? How will you spend your time?

WHERE?

Business: Local, regional, national, or international?

Customers: Where are they? What cities, states, countries?

Business Operations: Headquarters, sales offices, manufacturing, etc.?

WHO?

Customers: Who are they? (most businesses have several types of customers)

Strategic Alliances: Who can you partner with?

Advisors: Who can provide professional and strategic advice and help you grow this business properly?

Creating the Company You Want

Don't worry about answering all of the questions; just try to capture your immediate thoughts.

WHEN?

Start-up: When will this business be operational?

Facilities: When will office/manufacturing/distribution space be required?

Systems: When must they be selected, tested, and operational?

WHY?

Owner: Why am I creating this business?

Customers: Why will they buy these products or services?

Investors/Bankers: Why will they invest/loan money to this business?

HOW?

Financing: How will this business be financed?

Culture: How do you want to interact with employees, suppliers, customers?

Personal Beliefs: How will your personal beliefs about business impact this business?

INTERVIEW EXERCISE

This exercise helps you envision the kind of company you want (and don't want) in terms of products and services, customers, and the work environment. Sometimes, it's easier to answer the questions on the right first. Have your planning partner lead you through this exercise.

What's the product or service?

Describe three characteristics of your product or service:

Describe three things your product or service WON'T DO:

Who's the customer?

Describe three characteristics of your BEST current or potential clients or customers:

Describe three characteristics of clients or customers you would be better off NOT SERVING:

What's the business environment?

Describe three characteristics of successful businesses you admire and WOULD like to emulate:

Describe three characteristics of businesses you WOULD NOT like to emulate:

Crafting Your Vision Statement

FOCUS EXERCISE

STEP 1: Create a vision statement by filling in the blanks below. Have another person read it back to you.

Vision Statement (first draft)

Within the next _____ years, grow _____
company name

into a successful ☐ local ☐ regional ☐ national ☐ international _____
type or description of business

providing _____
description of products and/or services

to _____.
describe your customers

STEP 2: Rewrite the vision statement above, modifying it using your own words:

_____

_____

_____

_____

_____

_____

STEP 3: Now write a wildly optimistic, no limits, outrageous vision statement!

Examples of Vision Statements That Work!

Vision statements are individualised and stylistic. Here are 8 statements written by small to mid-sized business owners, with comments about what works well for each:

Sounds intriguing and innovative. Playful and yet stimulating. It's a large vision but very believable.

Create a network of Creativity Cafes around the world that are live and cyberspace networking salons featuring educational entertainment and electronic cyber theater. A fun place where people gather for play and work; where creative people, using the marriage of art and state-of-the-art technology learn from each other and have a forum for showcasing their work.

Creativity Cafe™ (www.creativity.com)

Narrative style. Personal, yet professional.

McAniff Consulting envisions a business that does excellent consulting work with small to medium clients in the Northwest and large companies nationally. The consulting work will emphasise the integration of the three "P"s of Planning, Process, and Performance to achieve excellent business results. My vision is to share office space and interact with other management consulting professionals to develop a successful practice.

McAniff Consulting

States specific information about what they will give to the community

The vision of Unity in Bedfordshire is to provide a loving and supportive diverse community which teaches practical Christianity and encourages spiritual growth and action. Within 3 years, 700 will attend 3 transformational Sunday services, and a mid-week, and monthly healing service. UIB will have 8 effective outreach programs across Bedfordshire. People will experience a deep sense of spiritual community, personal transformative growth and service to others as a path to God.

Unity in Bedfordshire

Offers a lot of information about the company. Includes elements of mission statement. States what is important to owners.

GeoCentral is a Napa-based company that is known globally for its:

- **Commitment to sharing earth's finest treasures by offering innovative products and services that showcase the richness and diversity of nature.**
- **Contribution for educating and promoting people's connection to this planet.**
- **Customer orientation, quality products, personal service, and retail earnings opportunity.**

Locally, GeoCentral is known for its beautiful, open, artistic offices, motivated employees, and community contributions.

GeoCentral (www.geocentral.com)

Very clear description of business. Appeals with humor.

To produce a weekly, wacky fun food show for national syndication where we take the everyday job of cooking and dish out some super easy, low-fat recipes and top it off with ladles of laughs. We want to become known as the Joan Rivers of cooking.

The ShortCut Cooks...

No-nonsense listing of what services will be provided

Within the next three years grow the Greater London Insurance Agency into a £15 million agency system with three locations providing auto, property and casualty, life insurance and financial services to individuals, families, and businesses that are concerned about being protected from the unpleasant and unexpected events of life.

Greater London Insurance Agency

Shows promising direction that company will move towards within a defined timescale

Over the next five years build ZXM Automation into the premier south coast industrial process automation consulting company specialising in integration solutions. ZXM Automation revenues will grow from £10 million in 2009 to £20 million by 2010 by expanding its role from a manufacturing representative company to a complete engineering field service and process solutions company.

ZXM Automation Consulting plc

Precise profile of client base outlined

By year-end 2010, grow Peter Smith at P. Smith Advisory Services into a £350,000 financial advisory service practice managing 40,000,000 in assets, providing trusted financial planning to 30- to 60-year-old clients for their retirement, and for their family's future wealth, who live in the West Sussex area.

P. Smith Advisory Services

FEEDBACK EXERCISE

Take a few days to reflect on the three vision statements you wrote on page 33. Then share them with a couple of friends or associates. Use this page to take notes and incorporate their feedback into your vision statement. ⌛ 60 minutes, 30 minutes per person.

First Person Feedback	Second Person Feedback

Note here key words and phrases from above or other sources you would like to use in your own vision statement:

Rewrite your vision statement below. Use your own style to describe your vision and choose words that are comfortable and meaningful to you.

Vision Statement

A Mission Statement That Works:

DaMert Company's mission is to create FUTURE CLASSIC products that capture…the wonders of the world around us, the magic of our imagination, the spark of innovation within each of us, and the mysteries of the future.

DaMert Company
(an international toy and gift company)

The Mission Statement

Why does this business exist?

Mission Statements always answer the question, "Why will customers buy this product or service?"

The mission statement describes the purpose for which your product, service, or business exists. Great mission statements are short and memorable. They communicate in just a few words the company's focus and what is being provided to customers. They always answer the question, "Why will customers buy this product or service?"

There is a current trend towards making mission statements very clear and focused. Often just a few words can truly describe a company's essence. For example, — Nike's Just Do It, Barclay's Fluent in Finance, No Limits, or FEDEX's The World On Time are powerful statements about their mission. While these examples are more typically considered tag lines or company slogans, they communicate volumes about these companies in just a few words. That's what a good mission statement should do. Your initial mission statement is likely to be multiple sentences, but try to keep it concise and powerful.

Mission statements are also about commitments and promises. Ask yourself, "What is your company committed to providing your customers or constituencies?" Under what circumstances would you refund your customer's money and apologise for not providing what was promised? What would you be willing to do to make amends with a dissatisfied customer?

The answers to these questions may help you to understand why your business exists. Consider them carefully.

Successful businesses balance meeting the needs of their customers with meeting their own needs. This balance is delicate, but it must be addressed in order for your business to succeed. Failure to define both your customer's and your needs may make the business equation out of balance. "Out of balance" can ultimately translate to "out of business" or being in a business that you don't like, want, or understand.

Mission statements are not about money. Include your financial goals in your vision statement and quantify them in the objectives, but leave them out of the mission statement. Pursuing an idea primarily to satisfy the need for money usually results in an unsatisfying business.

Mission statements must reflect the owner's passion and commitment. When the business satisfies an owner's passion for creativity, independence, or the need to serve others, there is substance and staying power in the mission. With a clear mission, you'll have the grounding necessary to see you through the tough times.
If you're not well grounded, you may abandon your company when the seas get too rough.

BRAINSTORM

EXERCISE

Your Mission...

Use these questions to reflect on why your business will be successful. Capture your thoughts using key words and short phrases.

1. What is the product or service? What differentiates you from the competition?

2. Describe your ideal customers.

What's in it for the customer and you?

3 Why will customers buy this product or service? What value does this product or service provide the customer? What unique benefits does this product or service provide the customer?

4 What passion(s) are you trying to satisfy by building this business? What beliefs do you have about business that will impact this business? What is the highest good that this business can achieve? What values will drive this business? Who will benefit from this business?

INTERVIEW EXERCISE

The interviewer writes down your answers to the questions on the left. As you ask the interviewer to restate what he/she heard you say, write your notes on the right. ⌛ 30 minutes

The Interviewer	You
Why will customers buy your company's product or service?	Answer restated:
What is your company committed to providing your customers?	Answer restated:
What can your company promise?	Answer restated:
What passion(s) are you trying to satisfy by building this business?	Answer restated:

Crafting Your Mission Statement

FOCUS

EXERCISE

Federal Express exists solely for one reason: Overnight Package Delivery.

Experiment with 1-6 key words that describe why your company exists from a customer point of view. Capture your competitive marketing edge or unique selling proposition.

1st Attempt

2nd Attempt

Does this mission support your vision?

Examples of Mission Statements

What works!		What doesn't!	
We are on a mission to help rescue people from heavy kitchen duty. The ShortCut Cooks (producers of a half hour comedy cooking show)	Short, fun, and right to the point.	**We will be one of the world's premier companies, distinctive and successful in everything we do.** AlliedSignal, Inc. (multinational materials manufacturer for aerospace, automotive industries)	Typical old corporate style. Not motivating, could be any company.
Partnerships in learning, research and professional practice. Blackwell Publishing	An eye-catching strapline	**To produce cars and trucks that people will want to buy, will enjoy driving, and will want to buy again.** Chrysler Corporation	Simple and straight-forward but could be more inspiring.
To help make South London a safer and more just place to live. South London Community Trust	Simple statement of purpose	**To exceed the expectation of our customers through the delivery of superior service and continuous quality improvement that rewards our employees and enhances the value of our shareholders' investment.** Total System Services, Inc. (a bankcard processing company)	Not memorable. Could be any company.
AUL's mission is to take care of people and their concerns about financial security. AUL provides peace of mind by sheltering its customers from the risk of loss caused by premature death, sickness, disability, or outliving financial resources after retirement. American United Life Insurance Company	This company cares about people, and their mission says how they can help.	**We produce and supply electricity, provide related products and services, and pursue opportunities that complement our business. We will continually improve our products and services to better meet our customers' needs and expectations, helping our customers, employees, owners, and communities to prosper.** Duke Power Company	Too long. Not inspiring. Full of platitudes. Could be many electrical companies.
We convert the spoken word to the written word with integrity. Jack London Court Reporters (a small court transcription company)	A powerful compelling statement.		
Healing, grounded in learning and supported by acts of personal kindness. University of California, San Francisco (a leading medical university)	Powerful message for all of the constituencies. The first mission statement was multiple pages.		

More Mission Statements

Personally made the way you want it.
A speciality, custom craft company

The purpose of the South West Region Business Club is to provide: education, networking, and support for new, prospective, and experienced entrepreneurs in the South West Region.
South West Region Business Club

We help you get out of bed feeling great so that you can experience the day the way you want to.
East West Healing Arts Center

To enhance the welfare of all retired people and to ensure that later life is a satisfying and enjoyable experience.
Seniors Priority Association

To enrich people's lives with programmes and services that inform, educate and entertain.
BBC

Total Reliability. No limits.
Tandem Computers

We move at the speed of business.
United Parcel Service

It's about communications between people... the rest is technology.
Ericsson (a global telecommunications company)

Create and sell unique software that transforms the way young people think.
Smalton Educational Software

We make our customers look great every day.
White Clothing Company

Help us lose weight. Recycle bimonthly.
Sacramento Waste Management

To connect young people of all backgrounds to learn about Hinduism in an unbiased environment.
Young People's Hindu Society

Bring light, air and the beauty of nature into homes through creative windows!
Hampshire Garden Window Company

Establish the Creativity Cafe as the New School for the Next Millennium. To inspire and empower the public in both cyberspace and in communities around the world by providing affordable access to technology and instruction and by creating experiences that inspire and educate us to be better human beings.
Creativity Cafe™

Helping people see better, one hour at a time.
LensCrafters

FEEDBACK

EXERCISE

Review your mission statements on page 43 and the examples on pages 44 and 45. Is yours too long? Unclear? Refine your mission statement below and then discuss it with two people. Use their feedback to complete your final version. ⌛ 60 minutes, 30 minutes per person.

Use the examples on the preceding pages to help you refine your mission statement:

First Person Feedback	Second Person Feedback

Rewrite your mission statement below. Experiment with different adjectives and verbs. It may help to move on to another section and come back to summarise your mission statement.

Mission Statement

Objectives That Work:

2009 Objectives for Sports Apparel Company...

Grow sales to £5.5m in 2009, £7.0m in 2010, and £9.0m in 2011.

Achieve profit before tax of £480,000 in 2009, increase to 10% of sales by 2010.

Introduce approximately 15 new products in 2009, achieving sales of £750,000.

Increase number of existing accounts with greater than £100m volume from 8 last year to 15 in 2009.

Secure two major product license agreements: NBA and NFL by 30/6/09.

Reduce shipping expense to 3% of sales, starting in 1st quarter.

Aggressively manage inventory to budgeted levels, maintain active inventory at 93%.

Reduce overtime to 3% of total manufacturing hours.

The Objectives

What are the goals? How does the business define success?

"Meaningful specifics *are those individuals who know what they want to achieve in very specific terms and have targets and time frames written down to help them get there.*"

Objectives clarify what it is you are trying to accomplish in specific, measurable goals. For an objective to be effective, it needs to be a well-defined target with quantifiable elements that are measurable.

Zig Ziglar, a motivational speaker from the US, says in order to achieve the goals that are important, you must become a *meaningful specific.* Meaningful specifics are those individuals who know what they want to achieve in very specific terms and have targets and time frames written down to help them get there. People who have vague ideas, with no target dates, never get to the finish line. Zig refers to these people as *wandering generalities.*

Whereas your vision statement is expansive and idealistic, and the mission statement short, powerful, memorable, and customer oriented, your objectives are designed to focus your resources on achieving specific results. The purpose of a well-defined objective is to cause meaningful action.

There are many types of objectives and your plan should include a wide variety. For many businesses the two most important categories will be the financial and marketing objectives. It is important, however, to tailor your objectives to cover the entire scope of your business, focusing on the goals that are most critical to your success.

Although there is no magical or precise number of objectives, The One Page Business Plan® can accommodate eight to nine different ones. If you have an objective for revenue, profitability, two or three for marketing, that leaves four or five to cover manufacturing, operations, personnel, and other important goals that are critical to your success.

Keep your objectives meaningful by making them specific and important. One of the most powerful aspects of the One Page Business Plan® is the limited amount of space. This requires prioritisation and pruning to get to a list of only the most important goals.

The exercises in this section are designed to help you analyse the important objectives for your business to achieve. The exercises will focus you on past successes and failures, as these are a great source of ideas for creating goals. The examples are designed to demonstrate how to construct powerful goals.

Create objectives that can be measured and then measure the results throughout the year. Objectives are a prime tool for accountability. Stay focused and stay on track!

BRAINSTORM

EXERCISE

What accomplishments would you like to celebrate...

Brainstorm three business accomplishments you would like to be celebrating at the end of this year and next year.

...this year?

...next year?

Imagine what you might say at the company celebration dinner:

CONGRATULATIONS!

We successfully completed (___)."

"We are proud to announce the beginning of (___)."

"We no longer have to deal with (___) because we (___)."

"We increased (___) by (___)."

We decreased (___) by (___)."

Where does success come from? What will it look like?

BRAINSTORM

EXERCISE

Think about your past experiences, what you have learned from these, and answer the questions on the left. Imagine what your future success will look like and respond to the questions on the right.

Where have you been successful in the past?

How can you expand upon these successes?

What were your past mistakes?

What have you learned from these mistakes?

What ideas have you not acted on?

Which of these ideas will you go forward with?

What targets will you aim for?

Check at least six objectives below that are critical for your success. Check as many in each category as you find to be appropriate and add your own if necessary.

Financial

- ☐ sales
- ☐ profit
- ☐ gross margin
- ☐ cash flow
- ☐ inventory
- ☐ owner compensation
- ☐ debt
- ☐ _____

Marketing and Sales

- ☐ image
- ☐ market share
- ☐ number of accounts
- ☐ number of customers
- ☐ number of new customers
- ☐ advertising
- ☐ visibility
- ☐ literature
- ☐ _____

Operations

- ☐ hours of operation
- ☐ number of locations
- ☐ suppliers
- ☐ shipping time
- ☐ customer service
- ☐ equipment
- ☐ _____

Human Resources

- ☐ compensation
- ☐ benefits
- ☐ safety
- ☐ morale
- ☐ environment
- ☐ overtime
- ☐ use of contractors
- ☐ volunteers (nonprofit)
- ☐ _____

Examples of Objectives

- Increase sales to £1 million in 2009, £1.5 million in 2010.
- Increase product margin to 42%.
- Reduce cost of goods sold to 28% by purchasing in bulk containers.
- Reduce number of days in receivables from 48 to 35 by 30/6.
- Reduce interest expense by 20% by renegotiating long-term notes.

- Introduce 4 new products in 2nd qtr; 6 in 3rd qtr; 2009 incremental sales £500,000.
- Launch new account incentive program in 3rd qtr; goal 50 new accounts generating £20k per month.
- Improve sales per employee to £120k per quarter by May 31st.
- Obtain one major new account per quarter generating £150,000 per year.

- Achieve billable time of 75%.
- Expand order entry access to 24 hours per day effective 30/6.
- Ship 98% of orders the same day and 100% of orders within 3 days.
- Produce and ship all special orders within 5 working days.
- Consolidate from 5 warehouses to 2 by 30/6; achieve annual savings of £500,000.
- Reduce customer service labour costs per order by 5% by 31/3/09.

- Hire general manager by 15/6.
- Reduce turnover to 3%; implement job rotation program by 1/1.
- Reissue updated employee handbook by 30/6.
- Develop scholarship program for employees' children by 1/9.

FOCUS EXERCISE

Use the examples of objectives below to help you decide which types of objectives are most important.

R & D

- ☐ new products
- ☐ introduction dates
- ☐ functionality
- ☐ image
- ☐ environmental
- ☐ design capabilities
- ☐ product improvements
- ☐ _____

Manufacturing

- ☐ production units/ cost
- ☐ capacity
- ☐ quality
- ☐ dual sourcing
- ☐ safety
- ☐ labour efficiency
- ☐ downtime
- ☐ inventory level
- ☐ _____

Personal

- ☐ role/involvement
- ☐ compensation
- ☐ creative needs
- ☐ retirement
- ☐ education
- ☐ personal growth
- ☐ charitable contributions
- ☐ public speaking
- ☐ _____

Other

- ☐ environment
- ☐ investors
- ☐ bankers
- ☐ suppliers
- ☐ government
- ☐ community
- ☐ _____
- ☐ _____

Examples of Objectives

- Complete clinical study No. 124 by 15/2.
- Develop prototypes for marketing samples by 15/1.
- Complete exploratory work on project *top cat* by 15/4; report available for management review 15/5.
- Decrease microbiology sample test costs to £1.50 per sample by 15/8.
- Automate laboratory documentation procedures by 15/6.

- Produce 1.3 million units in 2009.
- Expand our packaging line to 2 million unit capacity by 31/12.
- Reduce production labour to 8% of sales by 31/12.
- Develop dual sources for household and hair care products by 15/8.
- Significantly improve plant safety; target no loss time accidents.
- Improve manufacturing yield to 98%; achieve savings of £450,000.

- Commit to working no more than 50 hours per week; play on most weekends.
- Increase vacation to 3 weeks.
- Read one book per month.
- Exercise at least twice a week.
- Lose 20 pounds by yr end; 5 pounds per quarter.
- Relandscape backyard.

- Host community business luncheon in 4th quarter.
- Create five-year plan by 30/6 and begin investigating new sources of capital funding.
- Complete buy/sell agreement with partners; begin business succession planning.
- Commit 10 hours per quarter to community service projects.

FOCUS

EXERCISE

What does this business need to accomplish?

Review the objective ideas you checked on the previous two pages. Choose four of them and answer the questions for each.

Describe the activity required:	What will happen and when?	What is the financial impact?

1 Type of objective:

2 Type of objective:

3 Type of objective:

4 Type of objective:

EXAMPLE Type of objective: R&D

Develop/introduce new products	A book 6/30; Audio CD 7/31	Sales of £10,000 in 3rd qtr; £20,000 in 4th qtr

Crafting Meaningful Objectives

FOCUS

EXERCISE

Now rewrite the objectives on the left into sentences or phrases combining your responses in the four columns. The first two objectives will always be sales revenue and profitability.

sales revenue objective:

profitability objective:

1

2

3

4

Will meeting these objectives accomplish your vision and mission?

example:

Introduce a book by 30/6 and an audio CD by 31/7, resulting in 2009 sales of £30,000.

Examples of Objectives

What works!		What doesn't!	
Increase sales 25% to £4 million in 2009; £5 million in 2010, & £6.3 million in 2011.	Specific, measurable.	Develop a sustainable business; minimise peaks and valleys.	Not specific. No way to measure.
Increase production from 10,000 to 15,000 units per month, effective June 1st.	Clear and very specific.	Develop strategic marketing alliances with key partners.	Not specific. Which partners? To achieve what?
Introduce new hair care line, 1st quarter, estimated 2009 sales of £250,000; skin care line 3rd quarter, estimated 2009 sales of £100,000.	Measurable, specific, financial impact known.	Develop and introduce new products to grow business.	Vague. Needs type of products, how many, and financial impact.
Improve overall product margin to 40% by reducing discounts on low volume accounts to 3%; enforce minimum new product margin target of 45%.	States goal and how it will be achieved.	Improve profitability and cash flow to support business growth.	Needs to be quantified.
Reduce overtime to maximum of 3%; introduce 401k by June 30th; implement recognition program by Sept. 30th.	Says how morale issue is going to be tackled and when.	Improve employee morale.	No way to measure. No statement of work to be done.
Reduce inventory to £950,000 by 30/6/09; maintain raw materials @ 1.5 months; finished goods @ 2 months.	Clear, measurable goals.	Reduce inventory levels.	Doesn't state the desired result. Might cause other problems.

Read your vision and mission statements again and rewrite your objectives below. Ask yourself again if these objectives will accomplish your vision and mission statements.

Objectives

Strategies for the 21st Century...

Price isn't everything

Lots of customers will pay extra for a helpful, well-trained staff. Ask Neville Johnson.

Attract the very best employees and give them a stake in the business

Give rank-and-file employees a vested interest in how a company performs. Intel does.

Think fast

Particularly in the high-tech world, move and evolve quickly. Learn from Netscape.

Superior Execution

A well-executed plan for a simple product will beat a poor implementation of a great product everyday.

Be visible, be a resource

Write articles, newsletters, books, web pages. Speak to any group that will hear you. Volunteer your time and expertise whenever you can.

Don't try to do it all

Specialise in what you do best. Contract or forget the rest.

The Strategies

How to Grow and Manage the Business

Strategies set the direction, philosophy, values, and methodology for building and managing your company. Strategies also establish guidelines and boundaries for evaluating important business decisions. Following a predefined set of strategies is critical to keeping a business on track.

"Following a predefined set of strategies is critical to keeping a business on track."

One way of understanding strategies is to think of them as "industry practices." Every industry has its leaders, its followers, and its rebels, and each has an approach for capturing market share. Pay attention to the successful businesses in your industry and you can learn important lessons. Miss an important lesson and your business may not even get off the ground.

Strategies are not secret. In fact they are common knowledge and openly shared in every industry. Pick up any industry's publication and you will know precisely what the industry's leaders have to say about the opportunities and how to capitalise on them. These leaders will also share their current problems and their solutions. This is critical information for building and managing your business.

In most industries there are four to six core strategies that the successful businesses follow. These core strategies are easy to understand, remain relatively constant over time, are used by market leaders, and result in growth and profitability.

Great strategy statements can be broad and yet create tremendous focus. When you have the right strategies for your business, they will probably last for several years with minor changes. A significant breakthrough in your industry, or a significant change in your business, can of course cause you to revisit your strategies.

A properly constructed set of strategies will define your business and keep it focused. For example, a Chartered Certified Accountant whose vision is to build a local practice would be significantly off track to accept international clients who would take him out of the country on extended trips. An upscale boutique targeting high-income clientele would not be wise to locate right next door to a T J Hughes.

Strategies must address both internal and external influences that are affecting or may affect your business. External strategies capitalise on opportunities to grow the company or overcome outside threats. Internal strategies address issues related to the business's strengths and weaknesses in the areas of culture, capabilities, efficiency, and profitability.

Strategies provide the answer to the question: "What will make this business successful over time?"

BRAINSTORM

EXERCISE

Key Elements to Building Your Business

Check the boxes that represent those topics *critical* to growing and operating your business. Refer to your objectives while making your selections. Feel free to add to the list.

- ☐ Market Presence
- ☐ Employees
- ☐ Distribution Channel
- ☐ Referrals
- ☐ Partners
- ☐ Shared Support Services
- ☐ Product Cost
- ☐ Product Uniqueness
- ☐ Technical Knowledge
- ☐ Trademarks/Patents
- ☐ Customer Service
- ☐ Board of Advisors
- ☐ Time Management
- ☐ Cash Flow
- ☐ Company Image
- ☐ Reputation
- ☐ Key Customers
- ☐ Quality
- ☐ Other People's Skills
- ☐ Capital
- ☐ Trade Industry Acceptance
- ☐ Location
- ☐ Visibility
- ☐ Number of Accounts
- ☐ Technology/Equipment
- ☐ Family Support/Money
- ☐ Strategic Alliances

Decide Which Strategies Are Appropriate for Your Business

Finding appropriate strategies for your business is not difficult. Much information is readily available to you for free or at minimal cost. Selecting strategies you can utilise is also not difficult.

Where do you find strategies specific to your business? Trade journals, local business newspapers, and national business magazines are great places to start. These publications are filled with current articles on industry trends in the critical areas of marketing, finance, and operations. They are usually short, concise, and written by industry experts. They describe the problems and opportunities with which the industry is struggling and the solutions that businesses are implementing. A review of the contents for the last few issues will certainly give you a solid perspective on what's important in your industry and how the leading edge companies are planning their futures.

If you are starting a business, you'll have access to some important information that you will want to seriously consider before proceeding. Also, if this is a new business, and it requires funding, you can be sure the lender will want to know how you are planning to address these issues.

Other people that know your business can be very helpful in identifying and selecting strategies. Your banker, accountant, attorney, vendors, and employees have a lot of insight into your business. Ask them for their thoughts.

Opportunities and Threats

RESEARCH EXERCISE

Review the last three issues of your industry's trade association journal and answer the questions below.

What opportunities exist?	How can we capitalise on them?

What threats exist?	How can we minimise the threats or turn the threats into opportunities?

Examples of Industry Issues

pricing	environment	economic	the public
customers	market	technology	taxes
suppliers	competition	media	import/export regulations
cost reduction	government		

FOCUS

EXERCISE

Who are your customers?

List and describe up to three categories of your BEST CUSTOMERS.

Use the words below to help brainstorm your customer descriptions:

age
sex
income
occupation
education
language
family size
countries
regions
size of cities
social class
lifestyle
personality
purchase frequency
purpose of purchase
brand loyalty
habits
hobbies

Use the following words to help brainstorm how you will promote and sell to your customers:

workshops
associations
newspapers
direct mail
outplacement agencies
referrals
partnerships
Internet
local retailers
television
radio
telemarketing
magazines
speaking
government agencies
trade journals

1

2

3

How will you promote and sell to them?

Where/how do these customers buy your products now? Where/how will they buy them in the future?

How do you plan to PROMOTE your products or services to these three categories of customers?

BRAINSTORM

EXERCISE

What's working in your company?

It's just as important to know what works in your company as what doesn't. Use the keywords list at the bottom to help you brainstorm if you get stuck. (For established companies only.)

What currently works well in my company?

How can we improve?

What doesn't work well?

How do we solve the problems?

management	employee benefits	flexibility	customer service
employees	overtime	yields	safety
business practices	internal controls	expense control	profit margin
facilities	product quality	communication	morale
	manufacturing capacity	inventory management	

Critical Issues Examination

FOCUS

EXERCISE

Select three critical issues that are limiting your company's growth, profitability, or effectiveness. This exercise helps you differentiate between symptoms and root causes so that you can see more clearly what needs to happen to achieve a permanent and effective change. (For established businesses only.)

List 3 issues or symptoms:	What is the root cause of this?	What needs to change?	How will results be measured?
EXAMPLE Back orders are excessive!	No sales forecast, and capacity is too low	Develop monthly sales forecast by product and expand packaging	Track output per week vs. planned output; monitor back orders daily

FOCUS

EXERCISE

How do we get from here to there?

What has made your company successful or limited its growth to date? How will you build on the successes and overcome the current limitations to achieve your vision?

	Current Business*	Vision
Success Factors		
Limiting Factors		

*Current business could be your business or industry

Crafting Meaningful Strategies

FOCUS

EXERCISE

From the focus exercise on the previous page, select up to five areas that are critical to building your company. Draft a strategy statement for each one below.

1

2

3

4

5

Do these strategies describe:

How the business will be built and managed?

How we will capitalise on market opportunities?

How we will solve our business' critical problems?

Examples of Strategies

What works!		What doesn't!	
Position company for strategic acquisition in 2009; build brands, identity, management team, and profits.	Sets the direction with the big picture and exit strategy.	Make money, limit investment in business and employees, think about retirement at age 65.	Everything is wrong with this strategy.
Sell total solutions, not time, not parts.	Selling value, not time. Allows for much higher margins.	Employees: hire at the lowest possible wages, perform important functions ourselves.	Great employees are worth their weight in gold.
Employees: hire the best, have them just before we need them, retain them through job satisfaction and equity participation.	Always need good people. Have a people strategy.	Ideal client: anyone who will buy our products and services.	It's impossible to be everything to everyone. Specialise.
Control expenses and growth; self-capitalise/bank finance company; achieve sales and profit plans.	Build a strong company with good internal controls.	Product: whatever is hot this year, we will sell.	Followers rarely have the volume or margin the leaders do. Invest in R&D.
Focus on web-based training and communications products with delivery via Internet, Intranet, CD- ROM.	Defined set of products. Clear and understandable.	Increase prices to maintain margins.	Might work in the short run. Competitors will find a way to do it better for less.
Aim high with minimum project size of £300,000.	Sets lower limits.	Project size: all projects.	Not all clients or projects are profitable. Refer low-margin projects to your competitors.

Use this summary to refine your strategies by writing them below. Check each strategy for the following characteristics: easy to understand, constant over time, used by market leaders, and results in growth and profitability.

Strategies

Strategies, Plans, and Objectives must be linked to each other!

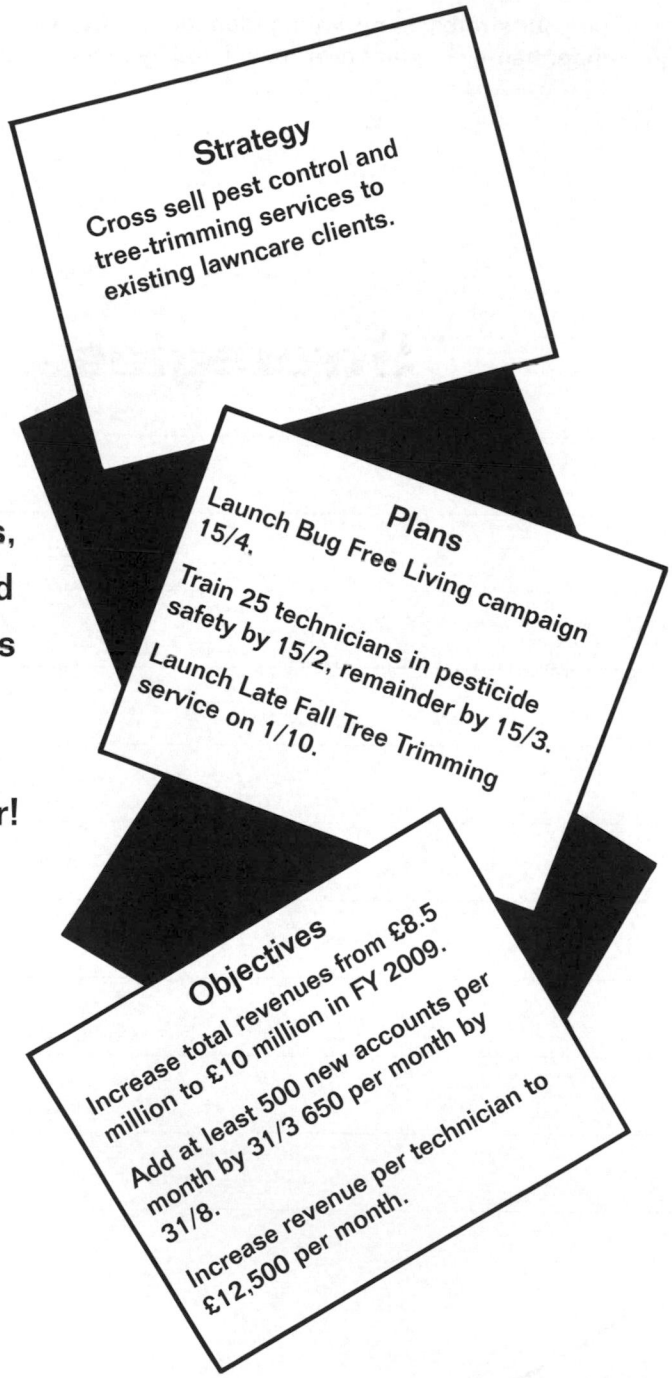

The Plans

What specific actions will the business implement to achieve its goals?

"It's not enough to talk about it... you must say how and why!"
— *Inc. Magazine* comment on business planning

Plans are the specific actions the business must implement to achieve the objectives. Plan or action items should be important, significant, and contribute to the growth of your business. Each plan or action item is, in effect, a project.

Ideally, each plan statement should directly relate to an objective and a strategy. Plans should be action oriented, should specify specific tasks, and should have deadlines. If your business has employees, independent contractors, or utilises outside resources to complete tasks, the ideal plan statement will identify who is responsible for performing each function.

Most business owners or prospective business owners have a to-do list a mile long. They struggle not with what needs to be done, but how to get it all done. The One Page Business Plan® is designed to keep you and your business focused on the important, but not necessarily urgent, business tasks. Steven Covey in *First Things First* writes about how easy it is to focus on the most important tasks every day and never get to the things that will really grow your business. By having your business-building action list clearly defined, and delegated appropriately, it becomes possible to complete the tasks that will build your business.

The exercises in this section are designed to guide you in the development and prioritisation of your action plans and in relating them to specific objectives and/or strategies. The exercises suggest that you prepare estimates of the financial or operational impact of each of these projects and determine in advance how you will measure the results. This process provides both an objective framework for selecting the projects with the highest benefit or payback and a method for postauditing the results.

In preparing your plans, estimate the cost and time frame for each project. Transfer this information into your budget worksheets, calculate the impact of your to-do list on your cash flow. I've learned that if you don't know what your projects will cost, it's quite likely you will not have enough cash to fund them. A project with no cash is like a car with no gas — it's not going very far.

Make your plans carefully. Execute them on time, within budget, and with excellence. Measure their impact routinely.

BRAINSTORM

EXERCISE

List six projects that would make a big difference in your business. Tie them to an objective or a strategy. Then answer the three questions for each project.

Strategy or Objective:	Strategy or Objective:
Project 1:	Project 2:

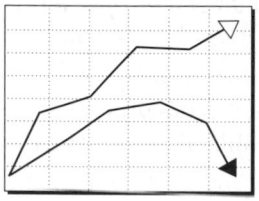

1. What impact would completing the project have?

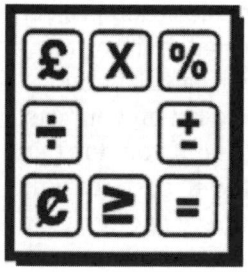

2. How will you measure the results?

3. What are the next three steps?

Business-Building Projects

Strategy or Objective:

Strategy or Objective:

Strategy or Objective:

Strategy or Objective:

Project 3:

Project 4:

Project 5:

Project 6:

FOCUS

EXERCISE

Integrating Objectives, Strategies, and Plans

Choose five projects from the preceding two pages and complete the chart below.

Objective or Strategy	Project to be Completed	Person Responsible	Completion Date
Plan 1			
Plan 2			
Plan 3			
Plan 4			
Plan 5			
EXAMPLE			
Increase sales volume 10% in 2009	Introduce new skin care line	M. Jones	30/6/09

Crafting Meaningful Plans

FOCUS

EXERCISE

Now rewrite the plans on the left into sentences or phrases, combining your responses in the four columns.

1

2

3

4

5

example:

Complete new skin care line and have ready for September 6th convention; M. Jones project team leader

Examples of Plans

What works!		What doesn't!	
Attend London trade show in June; Birmingham in September; and Manchester in October.	Identifies specific activity with dates.	Write annual employee reviews for R. Smith and B. Jones by 28/2.	Important activity but not a task that builds the business.
Complete phase III network design by 31/7. Utilise Suffolk Software, plc. for QA review.	States work to be completed with completion date; identifies vendor.	Complete February financials by 15/3.	Routine activity; this is not a strategic business activity.
Overhaul skin care emulsion equipment during June shutdown.	Concise statement of time frame.	Implement new business practices.	Not specific; no dates and no accountability.
Hire route salesman for Ipswich area in fourth quarter.	Specific position; some leeway for completion.	Hire approximately six new employees.	All new hires should be identified by position and approximate hire dates.
R. Smith to complete grant for handicap access upgrade by February 28.	Clear accountability and responsibility.	Develop committees for fund-raising.	When? Who is responsible?
Redo tax seminar marketing brochures in 2nd quarter. Bob Jones to lead team.	Specific with accountability.	Increase all prices during this year.	Not specific; should identify specific products. Percent increase should agree with budget assumptions.
Move to new Acton facility October 15th.	Simple statement; allows others to plan accordingly.		

Use this summary to refine your plans by writing them below.

Plans

"He who chooses the beginning of a road chooses the place it leads to. It is the means that determine the end."

— Harry Emerson Fosdick

You Did It!

You Did It! Congratulations! Your plan is now in writing. You are feeling a major sense of accomplishment. Go ahead and celebrate. This was hard work. Having your plan, in your words, on one page is a powerful business tool.

At this time you should have a final draft of your One Page Business Plan® in your word processor. Step back and review it. How does it look to you? If you are like most people, parts of your plan feel very tight and others still need some work. That's normal and OK. As you have learned by now, this process is iterative. Use the checklist on the following page to help make any minor editing changes that are necessary and you are ready to start sharing the complete plan. This is polishing; do not do a major rewrite at this time.

Polishing Checklist

Now that you have your plan in a final draft form, it's time to put it to work.

You clarified and organised your thoughts into a concise business plan. Now others can respond to your plan.

Overall Review

- Do the key words and short phrases describe the essence of your plan?
- Does your vision feel big, expansive, and exciting?
- Is your mission statement powerful?
- Are your objectives specific and measurable?
- Do your strategies state how you are going to build and manage this business over time?
- Are your plans action oriented and will they accomplish this year's objectives?

Order and Abbreviation
(Edit objectives, strategies, and plan statements to one line)

- Eliminate all unnecessary words and phrases.
- Abbreviate words when necessary.
- Use symbols like "&" in lieu of "and" to save space.
- Use "k" or "m" for thousands, "M" for millions.
- Communicate the importance and priority of objectives, strategies, and plans by placing the most important ones first in each section.

Creative Considerations
(especially with layout of vision and mission statements)

- Split sentences into multi-lines.
- Centre text.
- Use bullets to make key points stand out.
- Double space to accent.
- Highlight key phrases in italics.

Strengthening Exercises

- Draft and edit vision, mission and strategy until they are enduring statements that resonate with you, your partners, your management team, and key employees.
- Refine objectives and plan statements until they are very specific, measurable, and define clear accountability.
- Drop low-priority items; remember "less can produce more."
- Ask others for their comments.

Putting the Plan into Action

Putting the plan into action is the most important step because the actions deliver the results you wanted when you started this process. For most entrepreneurs, this is easy. You are action oriented and can't wait to get started. Now is the time to put the plan to work. A few guidelines or suggestions for uses of the plan are summarised below:

Use it to talk with your banker about financing.
Most bankers who have reviewed The One Page Business Plan® have found it to be an excellent tool for understanding both the business and the plans. It won't always lead to a loan being approved, and does not complete all the steps of the loan process, but it is an excellent start. Sharing your plan with your banker will get you useful feedback and lead to improved banker relations.

Discuss your plan with investors.
Your completed One Page Business Plan® is an excellent tool for focusing discussions with present or potential investors. The plan shows what you intend to do and how you will make it happen. Combined with your enthusiasm and commitment, the plan will be a significant aid in getting investors and keeping them happy.

Convert the plan into budgets.
Putting the plan into action usually requires quantifying the plans and objectives and getting the resources into place to support implementation. This is the process of budgeting. For many of my clients, this means going through the process of First Time Budgeting. Don't be afraid of it! Budgets help define the resources we need and provide the measures that allow us to know we are on track. If you need help in budgeting, get it. This is an important part of your path to success.

Manage the implementation.
Planning is a vital first step toward success but not the last step. Implementing the plan and making it work is the vital next step. More companies fail because of *Failure To Implement* than for any other reason. Managing the implementation is the process of using the goals, plans, measures, and other tools that we have defined and making sure that the actions take place and are in line with the defined strategies, objectives, and plans. Everyone must be held accountable for meeting their goals. Frequent reviews and continuous monitoring of results will help move you toward the defined goals. *Failure To Implement* is not acceptable and must be dealt with immediately.

External Presentation

- Complete business plan for small to mid-size companies
- Vehicle for testing business ideas with your board of directors, partners, banker, and employees
- Draft concept for Small Business Administration loan or venture capital funding business plan
- Summarises existing plan

Inspiration and Motivation

- Tool to get back on track if you've lost your vision
- Career planning

R&D

- Place to summarise ideas for new division or new business
- Quick sketch and fleshing out of idea for new product or service
- Process for planning major projects

Internal Process Guide

- Complete business plan for small to mid-size companies
- Business plan for subsidiaries or divisions of larger corporations
- Functional or departmental planning tool (sales, marketing, finance, etc.)
- Strategic planning starting point for CEOs in larger corporations
- Methodology to quickly update annual plan for significant mid-year changes
- Summarises existing plan

Keep the plan with you.

Update it with new thoughts.

Share it with people you trust and whose opinions you value.

Measure your progress at least quarterly.

Prepare a budget to match the plan.

Make a copy for everyone.
Have them post it on the wall of their office. Plans need to be communicated and understood to help drive the necessary decisions and actions that will lead to success. Certainly, all your managers and employees should have a copy of your plan. Others you may want to share it with could include your advisors, bankers, accountants, suppliers, key customers, and key community members. Share it with anyone who could help your business succeed. Remember that communities support entrepreneurs, but they must first know about you to support you.

Review your plan at team and company meetings.
Get some energy going around it. Implementing the plan means paying attention to it. Don't let it sit on a shelf. Your One Page Business Plan® is a working document that will work for you if you continually use it to remind your team and your employees about where you are going and how you will get there.

Use it as a decision-making tool.
Managers make decisions on the fly every day. The One Page Business Plan® is the guide they should use to make those decisions. Does the proposed action support where the company is going? How would we decide on this item based on the plan? The strategies, objectives, and plans are very clear guides on where resources should be used and what the priorities should be. The vision and mission are more general guides that help determine the overall direction and the values and principles that apply. The plan as a whole is the prime decision making document that should be checked when key business decision are made.

Useful plans drive decisions and actions and get everyone working toward the same goals. Decisions and actions that help implement the plan are positive and support the success of the company. Decisions and actions that go in different directions significantly reduce the probable success of the business. We plan in order to focus our actions and decisions to achieve the desired results. Words which sum up The One Page Business Plan® process are:

Focus → Action → Results

The plan provides the focus, and then we implement through actions guided by the plan. The planned actions lead to the results. When in doubt at this point, act. Sometimes try several actions, monitor the results quickly and carefully, and then decide on the best course of action to continue.

One Page Business Plan® Samples

As you modify your plan over time, use the following pages of sample plans to give you ideas for refining your content or design.

PeopleAssets

Innovative Consulting and Training Services for Tomorrow's Businesses

vision

Within the next 3 years, grow CGP into a £3 million national consulting firm specializing in creative leadership development programs for FTSE 100 companies.

mission

We help companies develop effective leaders!

objectives

- Increase revenue to £1.8 million in FY 2009.
- Increase gross margin to 54% from 31% by 31/12/09.
- Earn a pretax profit of £450,000 for FY 2009.
- By 31/12/09 establish a client base of at least 10 companies.

strategies

- Leverage CGP's worldwide identity as entree into business consulting.
- Build company awareness by networking at executive level.
- Create simple, easily-produced materials from existing CGP products.
- Use first clients to define product offering/build momentum.
- Use a train the trainer approach to maximise reach in larger clients.
- Create product ranges so that any business can afford a system.

plans

- Develop a written marketing plan by 16/2/09.
- Trademark Core Group Process by 4/4/09.
- Publish 4 quarterly newsletters; send to the first 1500 prospects by 15/3.
- Deliver 5 workshops by 30/6; and another 4 by Q3.
- Create high quality company brochure by 1/7/09.
- Create 4 mini-books on personnel management techniques by 31/12.

Z - TEC, plc.

vision

Within the next three years build Z-TEC International into a £50 million enterprise software solutions company specialising in integrated work-flow management solutions for large industrial process firms.

mission

Streamline the flow of work...in large industrial production facilities!

objectives

- Grow 2009 Revenue 20% to at least £27 Million.
- Achieve 2009 Profit before Interest & Taxes of £3.5 Million.
- Complete at least 8 new installations; yield fees of £6 million.
- Obtain 16 new clients w/ average project size of £500,000.
- Reduce accounts receivables from 63 days to 40 days by April 30th.
- Migrate at least 20 existing clients to web-product by Sept. 30th.
- Reduce employee turnover from 25% to less than 10% by Q4.

strategies

- Growth: 50% each yr by developing new clients & migration of existing clients.
- Reputation: Product leadership & reputation from existing client referrals.
- Partners: Align w/ industry leaders, partner for mktg & new products.
- Competitive Position: Optimise user-based pricing & modular system for flexibility.
- Products: Configure more than customise, business rules vs. custom programs.
- R&D: Work-flow solutions, open systems, multiple environments, object oriented.
- Resources: Have people & systems resources in place before they are needed.
- Aligned team, know the plan, sense of urgency, responsibility/accountability.
- Use Employee Incentives to share rewards, create excitement & have Fun.

plans

- Implement financial reporting system at project/dept level by May 31st.
- Establish Software Forum for sharing project mgt. & tech. issues by June 30.
- Measure progress against the business plan and allow for quarterly updates.
- Develop Sales & Marketing Resource Plan by 3rd quarter 2009.
- Develop partner strategies w/ Oracle, Sun Micro, IBM by Oct. 31st.
- Implement Professional Skills Programs in Nov.; Mgt. Development in Dec.
- Complete sales showroom remodel by Aug. 15th.
- Implement contractor peakwork load program by Sept. 15th.
- Upgrade internal systems including server, network, workstations by Dec. 31.

A high-tech company

All-Right Engineering, Ltd.

VISION:

Develop economically viable solution to 6782 printer memory error problem.

MISSION:

Reduce the incidence of printer fatal error messages.

OBJECTIVES:

Achieve .0000032 per thousand memory errors per average test cycle by 1/9/09.
Keep cost of upgrade to £1.53 per shipped unit.
Operate within budget of £356,000.00.

STRATEGIES:

Use 3 teams of 2 engineers plus 2 outside consultants.
Concentrate on fixing current design rather that replacing it with another.
Hold weekly progress meeting with team to review progress against plan/budget.
Use outside consultants on as needed basis for new laser technologies.

PLANS:

Establish teams by 1/3.
Identify and qualify 2 outside consultants by 1/3; finalise contracts by 1/3.
Complete problem assessment by 31/5.
Propose an engineering solution by 30/6.
Complete prototypes by 31/7.
Complete product trials by 30/8.
Document final product specs by 30/9.
Complete installation of modified production equipment by 30/11.

A management-consulting firm

Synergen Associates, plc.
Management Team Development Process

Vision

Within the next 12 months, evolve the existing management team into a vital growing force that:

- Fuels the growth of the company by seeing and being a part of the larger vision.
- Builds on its own energy and successes; learns from its failures/shortfalls.
- Expands capacity to contribute to the overall management of the company.
- Develops an espirit de corps that is supportive of the individual, the team, and the company.
- Design work style/culture that is adaptable/flexible to move quickly to meet customers needs.

Mission

Build a management team that builds the business.

Objectives

- Improve quality of decision making (measurement to be determined).
- Decrease amount of time to achieve management buy-in on key projects (measurement TBD).
- Reduce average time in management meetings from 25 hours/month to 12.
- Reduce average work week for management from 60 hours to 45 hours.
- Increase internal promotion ratio from 5% to 25%.
- Decrease management turnover from 20% a year to 5%.

Strategies

- Evolve the management team over time; do not go for immediate, but temporary fixes.
- Encourage growth/participation; do not push team faster than they can grow.
- Transfer skills from president to mgt. staff; provide training and coaching as required.
- Allow for small errors, learn from all mistakes, and celebrate the successes.
- Minimise fanfare about the process; let team respond to positive, subtle changes.

Plans

- Implement business planning and budgeting process starting on Nov. 2nd.
- Design and implement financial reporting system at Level 2 by Jan. 31st.
- Implement monthly business review sessions starting 2/24.
- Utilise CGC Consulting Group to facilitate quarterly development meetings starting Mar. 15th.
- Implement new managers training program in June; New supervisors training in Aug.
- Complete development of new employee orientation web-based learning module by 9/30.

Management Development

South West Region Business Club

the Association for Self-Employment Success!

VISION

Build SWRBC into a regionally recognised micro-enterprise organisation with an extensive greater South West Region network of entrepreneurial support groups providing nationally recognised products, programs and services to entrepreneurs, small-business owners, and partner organisations.

MISSION

The mission of the South West Region Business Club is to positively impact the community by creating viable businesses and successful entrepreneurial leaders through networking, support and connection to resources.

OBJECTIVES

- Increase total revenues from £125,00 to £350,000 in FY 2009
- Increase membership from 500 to 750 by December 31st.
- Launch 4 networks by June 30th; 6 additional networks by Dec. 31st.
- Generate £35,000 from entrepreneurial programs, events and products in FY 2009.
- Conduct 24 workshops/programs generate £18,000 in gross profit.
- Conduct 4 Corporate Connection programs with 400 attendees; generate £8,000 profit.
- Increase low-income/minority memberships from 50 to 100 by Sept. 30th.
- Award 10 scholarships totaling £10,000 in FY 2009.

STRATEGIES

- Use public relations and media to share successes, educate, recruit, and fund SWRBC.
- Market and sell SWRBC endorsed products and services nationally.
- Collaborate with natl micro-enterprise org. in national awareness programs and funding.
- Establish SWRBC centre to create long-term community presence & financial asset base.
- Attract/retain low-income entrepreneurs by offering scholarships funded by corp. sponsors.
- Utilise multi-lingual/cultural programs to attract minority entrepreneurs.
- Package successful SWRBC programs & products to sell to other micro-enterprise organisations.
- Use technology to manage growth, streamline operations, deliver programs, & sell products.

PLANS

- Complete funding plan by March 15th. Raise £100,000 by Jun. 30th.
- Hire executive director by May 15th.
- Expand board of directors from 5 to 9 by Aug. 31st.
- Develop SWRBC product and service marketing plan by Sept. 15th.
- Develop 2-year network expansion plan by Oct. 31st.
- Launch sales/marketing plan of One Page Business Plan by Nov. 15th.
- Collect /write 20 success stories by Aug. 1st. Implement public relations plan by Nov. 1st.

A nonprofit association

West Country Knits
2009 Business Plan

Vision

West Country Knits is a creative, soul-filled enterprise that provides:

- vibrant, unique, comfortable clothing as art for women.
- custom design capabilities for individual clients.
- training and mentoring of the next generation of machine knit artists.

Mission

To provide colour, light, and energising beauty
in comfortable, natural fiber clothing.

Objectives

- 2009 Revenue £150,000.
- Achieve profit margin of 50% by holding production labour to 18%.
- Increase active store count to 20, an increase of 30% over 2009.
- Outsource 50% of production by 4th quarter.
- Add three new designs; 2 ready-to-wear, 1 gallery collectible.
- Attend at least six trade/trunk shows in 2009; yielding sales of £40,000.

Strategies

- Produce gallery quality garments to attract high-end consumers, galleries, & collectors.
- Design products w/ multiple price points; attract attention w/ gallery quality garments, but have affordable products available at £150 – £200 price point.
- Build network & professional relationships w/ in fashion & garment industry.
- Outsource ready-to-wear lines, reserve personal time to create one-of-a-kind garments.
- Develop professional team for production and operation of business.
- Cultivate relationships with upscale clients for referrals and shows.
- Explore avenues to entertainment industry for costume and personal clients.

Plans

- Develop budget and plans for capital needs for business (4/09).
- Complete 2 ready-to-wear designs for show in Cheltenham in April.
- Contact six (list attached) fashion magazines; present portfolio for publication.
- Submit 10 applications (list attached) for retail and wholesale craft fairs (2/09).
- Attend three trade shows: London, June; Bath, August; Bristol, October.
- Continue to send garments to consignment galleries where advantageous.
- Complete redesign of display booths for fairs by March 15th.
- Hire interns or apprentices for in-house production, maintenance, office work (2/09).

A speciality manufacturing company

Universal Electronic Controls, plc. — Business Plan

VISION

To build Universal Electronic Controls, plc. into the premier industrial process control company in the Southwest by expanding its role from a manufacturing rep. company to a valued-added rep. company offering complete engineering, field service, and integration engineering services.

MISSION

UEC's mission is to help its clients control their processes and to provide an effective marketing, sales, service, and distribution channel for its manufacturers.

OBJECTIVES

Grow business 20% & achieve total sales revenues of £8 million in 2009.
Secure at least £500,000 in muni contracts in 2nd Qtr.
Land at least 8 system projects at a minimum of £100,000 each in 2009.
Increase gross margin from 14.8% to 15.5%.
Achieve net profit of £300,000, an increase of 50% over last year.
Increase sales per employee from £500,000 to £600,000.
Reduce Accounts Receivables from 58 days to 40 days by June 30.

STRATEGIES

Sell total solutions, not parts.
Build value-added services capability: engineering, service, eng. integration services.
Expand market geographically into London and the South East.
Aggressively target muni market & large scale processing manufacturers.
Increase margins by selling bundled parts & service; make cust. support a profit centre.
Increase outside sales force effectiveness by strengthening sales support function.
Control expenses & growth, self-capitalise/bank finance, achieve sales & profit plans.
Develop autonomous, self-directed & controlled management team.
Share growth & prosperity w/ employees through incentive & equity participation.

PLANS

Complete 2009 business plan & budgets.
Write business plan for Bristol muni contract - 1st Qtr.
Develop marketing program for major systems sales - 1st Qtr.
Organise & staff sales territories; reduce discounts from 5% to 4% - Jan. 09.
Hire Tech Support Mgr. & Service Group Mgr. in 1st Qtr.
Purchase South East company or develop plan to expand w/ internal resources - 1st Qtr.
Develop incentive comp. programs for sales support & key employees - 1st Qtr.
Host two user seminars for key clients: April & Sept.

A distribution / manufacturing representative company

Custom Business Interiors
2009 Business Plan

Vision

Build a successful business furniture company that specialises in providing competitively priced furniture with superior service to companies with 10 to 50 employees.

Mission

To provide growing companies a single source for purchasing all of their office furniture and equipment from an experienced professional that understands how to create attractive, functionable, flexible, and affordable office layouts.

Objectives

- Generate sales of £500,000 and profits of £100,000 in 2009.
- Increase gross margin from 28% to 35%.
- Increase No of orders at £10,000 level to 50% of business.
- Conduct 15 "workspace efficiency" workshops for small businesses.
- Limit personal work time to 40 hrs; will hire assistant in Feb.

Strategies

- Build reputation for excellent service; become the Neville Johnson of office furniture.
- Focus on growth companies in Greater London, Birmingham, and Manchester.
- Target market to financial institutions, insurance & computer companies.
- Keep competitive price advantage by keeping overhead low.
- Sell via catalogs and does not invest in showrooms or inventory.

Plans

- Complete revised marketing brochure & mail to existing clients Jan. 31st.
- Complete research on two new suppliers by June 09; annouce in Aug.
- Add PC-based design and layout software in May; announce in Aug.
- Redesign ACT! database by April to simplify direct mail process.
- Notify network by Jan. 15th regarding hiring plans for assistant.

A business-to-business product/service company

E Management Book

VISION

Become nationally known author, publisher, and consultant
serving entreprenuers and independent business owners.

~

- Consult primarily in Greater London Area; approximately 30% of my time.
- Create products (books, tapes, CDs) for the entrepreneurial market (25%).
- Speak extensively regionally, building to national recognition.

MISSION

Simplify the business of business for entrepreneurs.

~

Create professional business tools,
for entrepreneurs that build strong businesses.

OBJECTIVES

Complete E Management book by 27/6; print 500 cc's in July.
Publish article in Growing Business Online by 31/12/09; Yield 50 inquiries.
Sell 2,000 books in 2009.
First FTSE 1000 client in 2009, yielding consulting revenues of £50k.
One national convention speaking engagement in 2009; 6 in 2010.
Ten registered/certified E Mgt. practitioners by 31/12/09.
Complete E Mgt. audio tape by 31/8/09; annual sales of £50,000.
Complete Breakthrough Business book w/R. Miller by 31/12/09; 1st year sales £25K.

STRATEGIES

Collaborate to complete; can't do this by myself... Always keep it simple!
Use network/personal contacts to create opports to speak, get reviews, articles published.
Self-publish to start, prove marketability, seek national publisher.
Continue to turn consulting processes into products; products into programs.
Create products & programs for others to sell that serve the entrepreneurial market.
Seek endorsements/approval/intros/quotes from noted authors, CEOs, SBA.
Build brand & corporate identity.
Exit strategy: sell to major publisher or business training company in 5 – 7 yrs.

PLANS

Develop publicity & marketing plan by 31/7.
Develop E Management practitioners program by 31/7.
Contract w/ Audio Design Productions for audio tape production 4/09.
Submit articles to Growing Business Online and Financial Times for Dec. publication.
Complete mailing to 250 trade associations by 10/09 for speaking engagements.
Schedule 4 meetings w/R. Miller to complete 2nd book; 9/15 & 30, 10/15 & 10/31.

A business plan for a product

Would you like to share your One Page Business Plan® with others?

Show us how well this process worked for you by sending us a copy of your One Page Business Plan®. Please be sure to include your contact details and responses to the survey on the following page.

The One Page  **Business Plan® Company**

The One Page Business Plan Company
1798 Fifth Street
Berkeley, CA 94710 USA

Fax: (510) 705-8403

feedback@onepagebusinessplan.com
www.onepagebusinessplan.com

Notes

Notes

Notes

The Entrepreneur's CD Toolkit
How to Install and Use the CD

Installation Instructions:

Simply load the CD into your CD drive. Requires Microsoft Word® and/or Excel® to use the templates, forms and spreadsheets. Open any Directory with a double-click. Select desired Word® document or Excel® spreadsheet.

CAUTION:

Immediately after opening any of the files we encourage you to save the file with a new name using the "SAVE AS" command in order to preserve the original content of the file.

No Technical Support

This CD is provided without technical or software support. Please refer to your Microsoft Word® or Excel® User Manuals for questions related to the use of these software programs.

System Requirements:

Windows 95/98/NT/2000/XP
Macintosh OS 9.1 or higher
Microsoft Word® and Excel®
CD/ROM drive

SOFTWARE LICENSE AGREEMENT

This is a legal agreement between you, the user, and The One Page Business Plan Company. This agreement covers the software that is distributed with this CD and any subsequent software that may be distributed to you from One Page in the form of additional CD's or the Internet.

By opening or breaking the seal on the Software packet(s), installing or downloading the Software, you agree to be bound by the terms of this agreement. If you do not agree to these terms, promptly return the this book and software to the place of purchase.

You may use one copy of the Software on only one computer at a time. If you have multiple licenses for the Software, you may use as many copies at any time as you have licenses. "Use" means loading the Software in temporary memory or permanent storage on the computer. Installation on a network server solely for distribution to other computers is not "use" if (but only if) you have a separate license for each computer to which the Software is distributed. You must ensure that the number of persons using the Software installed on a network server does not exceed the number of licenses that you have. If the number of users of Software installed on a network server will exceed the number of licenses, you must purchase additional licenses until the number of licenses equals the number of users before allowing additional users to use the Software.

LIMITED WARRANTY

The One Page Business Plan Company warrants that the Software disks will be free from defects in materials and workmanship under normal use for ninety (90) days from the date you receive them. This warranty is limited to you and is not transferable. Any implied warranties are limited to ninety (90) days from the date you receive the Software. Some jurisdictions do not allow limits on the duration of an implied warranty, so this limitation may not apply to you. The entire liability of The One Page Business Plan Company and its suppliers, and your exclusive remedy, shall be (a) return of the price paid for the Software or (b) replacement of any disk not meeting this warranty. This limited warranty is void if any disk damage has resulted from accident, abuse, or misapplication. Any replacement disk is warranted for the remaining original warranty period or thirty (30) days, whichever is longer.

The One Page Business Plan Company does NOT warrant that the functions of the Software will meet your requirements or that operation of the Software will be uninterrupted or error free. You assume responsibility for selecting the Software to achieve your intended results and for the use and results obtained from the Software.

The Software is protected by United States copyright laws and international treaties. You may make one copy of the Software solely for backup or archival purposes or transfer it to a single hard disk provided you keep the original solely for backup or archival purposes. You may not rent or lease the Software or copy the written materials accompanying the Software, but you may transfer the Software and all accompanying materials on a permanent basis if you retain no copies and the recipient agrees to the terms hereof.

THE ONE PAGE BUSINESS PLAN COMPANY DISCLAIMS ALL OTHER WARRANTIES, EXPRESS OR IMPLIED, INCLUDING, BUT NOT LIMITED TO, IMPLIED WARRANTIES OF MERCHANTABILITY AND FITNESS FOR A PARTICULAR PURPOSE, FOR THE SOFTWARE AND ALL ACCOMPANYING WRITTEN MATERIALS.

This limited warranty gives you specific legal rights; you may have others, which vary from jurisdiction to jurisdiction.

IN NO EVENT SHALL THE ONE PAGE BUSINESS PLAN COMPANY OR ITS SUPPLIERS BE LIABLE FOR ANY DAMAGES WHATSOEVER (INCLUDING, WITHOUT LIMITATION, DAMAGES FOR LOSS OF BUSINESS PROFITS, BUSINESS INTERRUPTION, LOSS OF BUSINESS INFORMATION, OR OTHER PECUNIARY LOSS) ARISING OUT OF USE OR INABILITY TO USE THE SOFTWARE, EVEN IF ADVISED OF THE POSSIBILITY OF SUCH DAMAGES.

Because some jurisdictions do not allow an exclusion or limitation of liability for consequential or incidental damages, the above limitation may not apply to you.

A whole bookshelf of business brilliance

978-1-841-12804-7

Perfect for: Getting a bank loan, securing credit, raising capital and planning your business

Business Plan IN A DAY

Rhonda Abrams and Guy Clapperton

Get it done right, get it done fast!™

978-1-841-12805-4

The information and inspiration you need to get your business up and running fast!

Six Week Start-Up

Rhonda Abrams

A step-by-step program for starting your business, making money and achieving your goals!

978-1-841-12807-8

'User-friendly and exhaustive...highly recommended' - Forbes Magazine

The Successful Business Plan

Rhonda Abrams and Paul Barrow

Secrets and Strategies

978-1-841-12808-5

Foreword by Scott Cook, Founder, Intuit Corporation, makers of Quicken

What Business Should I Start?

Rhonda Abrams and Paul Barrow

7 Steps to Discovering the Ideal Business for You

978-1-841-12806-1

Sales presentations, classes, speeches, seminars, meetings of all sizes!

Winning Presentation IN A DAY

Rhonda Abrams and Guy Clapperton

Get it done right, get it done fast!™

Includes fast and easy starter guide to Microsoft® PowerPoint®

- Develop a powerful presentation and deliver it with impact
- Learn the secrets of experienced professionals
- Quickly become a PowerPoint® pro

CAPSTONE

be inspired!™

An Imprint of WILEY

Now you know.

Also available from Capstone

ISBN 9781841124704

ISBN 9781906465049

ISBN 9781841127941

ISBN 9780470694442

ISBN 9781906465254

ISBN 9781841128030

CAPSTONE
be inspired!™
An Imprint of WILEY
Now you know.

DAY
OOK

WITHDRAWN

157144